National
Audubon
Society

CONCISE
BIRDFEEDER
HANDBOOK

National
Audubon
Society

CONCISE
BIRDFEEDER
HANDBOOK

ROBERT BURTON

A DK PUBLISHING BOOK

Editor Candida Ross-Macdonald
Designer Phil Kay
U.S. Editor Jeanette Mall
Managing Editor Krystyna Mayer
Managing Art Editor Derek Coombes
Production Antony Heller

First American Edition, 1992
2 4 6 8 10 9 7 5 3 1
First Concise Edition, 1997

DK Publishing Inc., 95 Madison Avenue
New York, New York 10016
Visit us on the World Wide Web at http://www.dk.com
Copyright © 1992, 1997 Dorling Kindersley Limited, London
Text copyright © 1992, 1997 Robert Burton

Material in this book was previously published under the title of
National Audubon Society North American Birdfeeder Handbook.

Library of Congress Cataloging-in-Publication Data
Burton, Robert [1941]
    National Audubon Society Concise birdfeeder handbook / by Robert Burton :
1st American ed.
        p. cm.
    Includes bibliographical references and index
    ISBN 0-7894-1465-1
    1. Birds, Attracting of. 2. Birds—Concise—Identification. 3. Bird feeders.
I. Title. II. Title: Concise birdfeeder handbook.
QL676. 5.B87 1992   91–58218
598'.0723473—dc20   CIP

Reproduced by Colourscan, Singapore
Printed and bound in Italy by Lego

CONTENTS

•

CHAPTER ONE

ATTRACTING BIRDS

BIRDS WILL VISIT your yard only if it offers them some of the basic necessities of life. Every bird needs three fundamental things: food, water, and shelter. The presence of these basics both increases the birds' chances of survival and encourages them to make more visits. If these provisions are not naturally available in your yard, there are many ways in which you can introduce them. Food put out in feeders plus nestboxes for nesting and roosting create a bird-friendly environment. This chapter describes various different feeders, the types of food you can put out, and birdbaths and nestboxes that you can make or buy. Guidance on constructing and siting equipment will help you to improve your yard for visiting birds.

A painted bunting takes seeds left out on a tree stump.

· WHAT BIRDS NEED ·

Y OUR SUCCESS IN attracting birds depends on how far you can fulfill their basic needs. Even if your yard does not contain a natural wealth of food, a water supply, or large, mature trees, you can create these features by providing food, feeders, birdbaths, and nestboxes. Knocking together pieces of lumber to make nestboxes and feeders is a good way for a novice woodworker to start and provides an outlet for the creative urge. Only a little practice and application are needed, and birds do not mind if construction is less than perfect. Your efforts will not take long and will be quickly appreciated.

FEEDING THE BIRDS

Confident caller *A male red-bellied woodpecker takes a nut from a hopper feeder. These woodpeckers are easily attracted, and many become quite tame.*

"Feeding the birds" ranges from throwing crusts from the kitchen window to supplying commercial quantities of food in a battery of feeders. Thirty million tons of seed are put out for birds every year in North America. This can be vital in winter or when there are young to feed.

The money and effort you put into feeding birds depends on your interest and the time you can devote to watching them. My feeder array is strategically positioned outside my study window. I check that there is always enough food to keep the birds coming throughout the day, so that they provide a welcome distraction. I am also making some studies of who uses the feeder, so I have every excuse to gaze out the window.

WINTER FOOD

It is often said that once you start putting out food for birds in the winter, you should not stop until winter is over, and that if you cannot guarantee a continuous supply, it is best not to start in the first place. This strikes me as unnecessarily strict, and I was glad to find that my opinion was shared by the assistant director of the Cornell University Laboratory of Ornithology. While food put out in feeders makes life much easier for birds in winter, and is a valuable contribution to their survival in hard

weather, no bird relies entirely on one source of food. In natural circumstances birds have to adapt to changing food sources, and their survival depends on quickly finding new supplies.

There are some situations where birds may become dependent on birdfeeders. In spring, before natural food is readily available, or in unusually hard spells of weather, when it is temporarily unobtainable, well-stocked feeders are lifesavers. These are short-term measures for the birds, however, rather than a lasting dependence. Feeders are also the mainstay for birds in new housing developments, where the yards may be rather bare. Birds do not, however, rely solely on one yard: they make regular rounds of the neighborhood. So if you are away on vacation, the birds will simply bypass the empty feeder until your return.

Where birdfeeders have been maintaining an unnaturally high bird population, a shortage of food could develop if the birds were to be suddenly forced back on to natural food sources – especially at the end of winter, when supplies in the wild are low. I suspect that we simply do not know enough about the winter feeding habits of many birds to make a strict ruling either way, but do not feel guilty if your feeders occasionally remain empty for awhile.

Welcome visitors *Goldfinches are dependent on seeds for most of their diet, and in winter they are frequent visitors to seed feeders.*

SUMMER FEEDING

Many people stop feeding birds at the end of winter, afraid that it will tempt migrants to stay behind when they should fly north. In fact, the birds may need extra food to put on the fat used as fuel for the journey. The same holds for feeding in the fall. In particular, hummingbirds may benefit from a nectar substitute in an early cold spell.

Fast food *Crusts of bread and scraps of high-protein cheese can provide a valuable snack for parent birds collecting food for their young.*

Many of the birds that do not migrate still leave the suburbs and return to the country to nest. Those that do remain in the yard increasingly turn to whatever natural food is available, and ignore feeders, but the yard cannot always be relied upon to be an adequate source of food. If you have coaxed birds to nest in your yard by putting up nestboxes, you should make sure that they have enough to eat.

People are often afraid that nestlings may be fed unsuitable food from a feeder, but in many species the diet of the nestlings differs from that of the adults. The parents can obtain their own requirements quickly and easily at the feeder, while finding the correct natural food for their offspring. Problems may arise when natural food is scarce, and the nestlings are stuffed with dry bread or peanuts, which can choke them. You can stop putting out food during nesting, but do start again when the fledglings appear. They will need the benefit of easy meals, and you may have the pleasure of seeing entire families of small birds together at the feeder.

WATER

A supply of water in a birdbath or pond provides another incentive for birds to visit your yard throughout the year. Birds need fresh water for both drinking and bathing, and it is as important in winter as in summer. Those birds that feed on juicy worms and caterpillars do not need to

Wash and brush *A cinnamon teal, a marsh-dweller that visits ponds, preens and oils its clean, wet feathers after a bath.*

Watering hole *Even the insect-eating eastern bluebird appreciates a cooling drink from a birdbath on a hot summer day.*

provide in your yard becomes a vital reservoir when frost and snow seal off natural supplies. Fresh drinking water is a valuable resource at these times, the alternative being to eat snow, which costs birds dearly in energy needed to thaw and warm it. Birds also continue to bathe and preen throughout winter. This helps maintain the insulating properties of the plumage, which are vital for the survival of birds in cold weather.

drink as much as those that live on a diet of dry seeds, but a supply of water is always welcomed by all birds.

The birdbath is obviously very popular during hot summer weather, when birds need to keep cool, and puddles and small pools have dried up. Birds do not sweat but pant to keep cool, evaporating moisture from their mouths and lungs rather like dogs. It comes as a surprise to many people that birds need a birdbath as much in winter as in summer. The water that you

Drinking fountain *A house sparrow, attracted by the sound of running water, takes a quick drink from a running faucet in a yard.*

NEST SITES

Even in a mature yard that is well planted with trees, dense vines, and shrubs, there is likely to be a shortage of suitable nest sites. This is especially true if large numbers of local birds have been maintained through the winter by food supplies at feeders, or if a zealous gardener has pruned the vegetation.

A few birds will nest in hidden corners and raise families. It is easier to follow the unfolding saga of birds' family lives if you put up well-placed nestboxes. These bring more birds into the garden and provide security so that nesting attempts are less likely to end in disaster. House wrens, chickadees, bluebirds, and other hole-nesting birds eagerly accept nestboxes, but other species, especially most members of the warbler family, do not use them.

A nestbox must be sited at least 6 feet (2 meters) above the ground, and away from the worst effects of the sun and rain, for example, under the shelter of a canopy of branches. It must be secure enough not to fall down, but it does not matter if it wobbles a little.

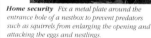

Home security *Fix a metal plate around the entrance hole of a nestbox to prevent predators such as squirrels from enlarging the opening and attacking the eggs and nestlings.*

Resist the temptation to visit a nestbox or any other nest. The laying period is a very sensitive time, and some birds desert their nests if disturbed. Visits also make the nest more vulnerable to predators who will follow the trail of your scent, out of curiosity. Research shows that a single visit to a robin or bluebird nest increases the chances of both desertion and predation. If well-grown nestlings are disturbed, they are likely to erupt out of the nest in a panic. If they do, gently place them back into the nestbox and stuff the entrance hole with a handkerchief until they settle down.

Natural appearance *Strips of bark nailed to the outside of a nestbox can make it more attractive to some bird species.*

11

· GARDENING FOR BIRDS ·

THE PROVISION OF food and places for birds to nest, drink, and bathe ensures that some birds will visit a yard. More time, money, and commitment are required if you want to make it a favorable habitat for as many birds as possible. It is easy enough to put up a feeder on the lawn and nestboxes in trees; it is another matter to plan, landscape, and plant the yard to encourage birds to visit and nest.

BIRDS AND PLANTS

It is hardly worth creating a bird habitat if your yard is a playground for cats or small children. You may also find it difficult to attract birds if you are a keen gardener devoted to growing the best flowers and vegetables, because a tidy yard does not provide the best food and shelter for birds. It is not usual practice to leave weeds like dandelions and thistles to seed, but that is the best way to attract pine siskins and goldfinches.

Flower feeder *Finches such as this purple finch sometimes strip buds in spring, a habit that looks destructive but does not appear to harm the plant.*

Most gardeners try to destroy as many plant-eating pests as possible. Apart from the danger of birds eating poisoned pests, remember that insects are especially important to birds feeding their young. A profusion of vegetation encourages the insects needed for successful nesting, yet no one pursuing horticultural excellence will grow plants as nurseries for caterpillars.

Unfortunately, you cannot rely on birds to control insects. Birds feed on the foods that are most abundant. When a swarm of aphids, for example, begins to dwindle, the birds search for something else, leaving plenty of aphids to carry on the infestation.

Double attraction *Goldfinches come to thistles not only to feed on the seeds, but also to collect the soft down, which they use in their nests.*

The best plan for any bird yard is to settle on reasonable compromise. Careful choice of plants and a little judicious laziness in weeding and tidying will create an environment that attracts a wide range of birds without making the garden unsightly.

If you have moved into a new home, what can you do to attract birds, apart from erect feeders and nestboxes? The creation of a bird habitat is within everyone's reach, although it takes some time, and may not be worth it unless you plan to stay where you are for awhile. It is largely a matter of letting the garden grow a little wild and choosing the right plants. Local nurseries and wildlife organizations can advise you on the plant varieties, or you can take a look at what is growing wild nearby.

Wild garden *Flowering and fruiting trees, long grass, and hedges allowed to grow wild all combine to create an ideal bird habitat.*

TREES

Trees are the most important feature for attracting many birds and are vital for woodpeckers, nuthatches, tanagers, and creepers. Choose trees that support plenty of insects and provide seeds or fruit. These include birches, maples, hollies, mesquite, mountain ash, palmetto, mulberries, and evergreen oaks. Black alder is fast-growing and good for fall migrants, and sumacs retain their seeds – eaten by pine grosbeaks and robins – through the winter.

Fruit trees provide food for both humans and birds, as well as attractive blossoms in spring. Cedar waxwings will even feed on apple blossoms. If you plant more trees than will provide your own needs and net part of the crop, then you will not mind the birds taking a share.

Trees also provide nest sites and cover from predators and weather. Evergreens on the windward side of a lot shelter the house and provide cover for birds, but even bare branches create a warmer environment in winter.

Ideal home A dead tree can be an asset, because birds such as flickers will nest in the hollow stumps of dead branches.

The ground under the trees can be planted with smaller, shade-tolerating trees and shrubs, such as dogwood, holly, and serviceberry, and a variety of ground-cover plants. This makes the yard habitat more like a natural grove and enhances its appeal to birds and people.

VINES AND SHRUBS

Trees take years to become established, so quick-growing vines form a useful stopgap and are useful for hiding walls and fences. Try honeysuckle, clematis, Virginia creeper, English ivy, wintercreeper, and grapevine. Some vines, like the trumpet creeper, have flowers that attract hummingbirds, others have edible berries, and all form dense growths that are good for nesting.

Shrubs are similarly useful for shelter and food and, unlike trees, provide these needs within a few years of planting. Good shrubs for attracting birds – especially thrushes, orioles, and vireos – include firethorn (pyracantha), cotoneaster, serviceberry, blackberry, and dewberry.

Be sparing when clipping shrubs. Dense growth provides the best nesting places, so wait until nesting has finished and the berries have been eaten before pruning.

High rise and low level Varied shrubs and ground cover will attract a wide range of birds that like to nest and feed at different heights.

High visibility
The bright red color of pyracantha berries is attractive to fruit-eating birds such as these cedar waxwings.

LAWNS

A lawn is similar to a clearing in the woods. It gives you a clear view to the surrounding trees and shrubs and attracts birds that like to feed in open spaces. Avoid using chemicals on the lawn.

If you are serious about attracting birds, weeds in the lawn will be very useful. If the lawn is allowed to grow a little long, the plants will set seed for doves, sparrows, and finches. You can leave the grass long around trees and in odd corners. It also shelters many small animals that other birds will hunt.

Watch the contrasting feeding styles of birds on the lawn. Robins hop and pause stealthily with head cocked to stare into the grass for the slightest movement of a worm or grub. Starlings stride about purposefully, thrusting their bills into the ground and squinting down the holes. Flickers search for ants and other insects with their long tongues. They will be joined by juncos, grackles, red-winged blackbirds, mockingbirds, ring-necked pheasants, rosy finches, horned larks, and meadowlarks, as well as bobwhites in the east and California quail in the west.

Home ground *Birds such as this eastern meadowlark feed and nest on the ground and will be attracted to longer grass.*

Watering your lawn in dry weather is a great help to the birds because it brings earthworms to the surface. Worms are a boon when there are nestlings to feed.

Soil at the edges of the lawn and around trees and shrubs is useful to seed-eating birds such as doves and gamebirds, which need to swallow grit to assist their stomachs with grinding their hard food – a mourning dove needs 150 grit fragments each day. Bare soil will also be used by all birds for dust-bathing.

Happy hunting *Although it is often seen, a robin hunting worms and grubs on a lawn is still a captivating spectacle.*

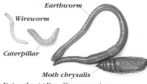

Natural supplies *The average lawn can harbor a surprising stock of foodstuffs, if it is left unpoisoned by chemicals.*

· FEEDERS ·

THERE ARE A wide variety of feeder types, suitable for all
tastes and situations. Making your own is much more fun,
and acceptable results can be produced with few tools and
minimal skill. Feeders bring birds up from the grass and out of
the cover of trees and shrubs, giving you the opportunity to
observe their excitement as they jostle for food.

SITING YOUR FEEDER

The simplest way of feeding birds is to
scatter food on the ground, but most of it
will be lost to scavengers or seized by the
larger, bolder birds. Food on the ground
also quickly becomes messy. For this
reason, elevated feeders are needed, but it
is worth putting out food on the ground to
divert undesirable visitors from the more
expensive food that attracts shyer species.

Remember that birds feed at different
levels. Feeders at various heights attract
more birds and lessen conflicts.

A sheltered southeast exposure gives the
best conditions in the morning, when birds
prefer to feed. Feeders should be near
shrubs and trees where birds can rest and
escape if a hawk appears, but should not
be immediately next to undergrowth
because this gives cover for predators such
as cats. A brush pile is useful if your
feeders are exposed. Feeders on or near the
windowsill are best for watching the birds,
but it may take time for birds to become
used to coming close to a house.

OPEN PLATFORM FEEDER

Although the old-fashioned platform is seen
less often these days, it is worth stocking
one with scraps or cheap food to act as a
beacon for passing birds.

Platforms can be a source of infection, as
a result of trampled food or droppings, and
should be cleaned regularly. Scrape out
debris, and scrub the feeder with a solution

of soapy water and a little household
bleach, but rinse thoroughly before putting
it out again. The feeder shown is a
commercial model, but you can make one
using fine mesh or plywood sandwiched
between wooden frames. Keep larger birds
out by covering the platform with 1-inch
(2.5-centimeter) mesh.

Mesh platform
*The mesh allows
rain to drain away
from the food, so
that it does not
become soggy.*

Support
*A platform feeder
should be mounted
on a post at least 6
feet (2 meters) high.
The post should be
made of metal and
may need a baffle
against squirrels
(see page 41).*

COVERED PLATFORM

You can use the base of this feeder alone as an open platform, or you can make a covered platform. The gaps in the edges on the base allow water to drain from the platform. A roof will keep the food dry and provide a place to hang a seed hopper.

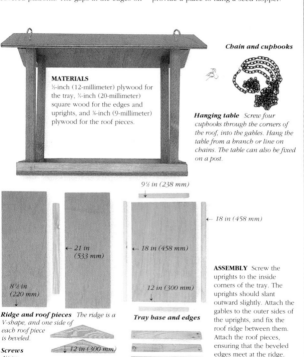

MATERIALS
½-inch (12-millimeter) plywood for the tray, ¾-inch (20-millimeter) square wood for the edges and uprights, and ¾-inch (9-millimeter) plywood for the roof pieces.

Chain and cupbooks

Hanging table Screw four cupbooks through the corners of the roof, into the gables. Hang the table from a branch or line on chains. The table can also be fixed on a post.

9½ in (238 mm)

21 in (533 mm)

18 in (458 mm)

8½ in (220 mm)

18 in (458 mm)

12 in (300 mm)

Ridge and roof pieces The ridge is a V-shape, and one side of each roof piece is beveled.

12 in (300 mm)

Tray base and edges

ASSEMBLY Screw the uprights to the inside corners of the tray. The uprights should slant outward slightly. Attach the gables to the outer sides of the uprights, and fix the roof ridge between them. Attach the roof pieces, ensuring that the beveled edges meet at the ridge.

Screws
1¼ in (30 mm)

Gables
2½ in (60 mm) high at center

Nails
1¼ in (30 mm)

Uprights 13 in (335 mm) with an angle at each end

SUET MIXTURE HOLDER

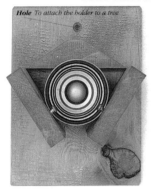

Hole To attach the holder to a tree

If you decide to make a suet mixture *(see page 29)* in an old food can, you can turn the "pudding" out onto a platform feeder, hang it up in a mesh bag or wire basket, or make a simple holder for the can. The holder can be nailed to a post or a tree trunk. It keeps the pudding dry and makes it last longer because it is difficult for birds to break off large chunks of the pudding and carry them away. The small screws in the side supports that hold the can in place are easily removed to release the can for refilling. To ensure that the top edge of the can is not jagged or sharp, use a can opener that leaves a smooth, blunt edge. This feeder holds a 16-ounce (450-gram) can; if you use a can of a different size, adjust the dimensions below accordingly, attaching the brace higher or lower to accommodate the diameter of the can.

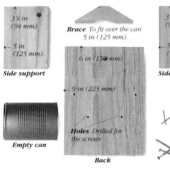

3¾ in (94 mm)

5 in (125 mm)

Side support

Brace To fit over the can 5 in (125 mm)

6 in (150 mm)

9 in (225 mm)

Holes Drilled for the screws

Empty can

Back

3¾ in (94 mm)

5 in (125 mm)

Side support

Small screws ⅝ in (15 mm)

Oval nails 1¼ in (30 mm)

Rust-proof screws 2½ in (60 mm)

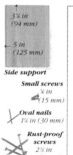

LOG FEEDER

Drill a few ½- to 1½-inch (13- to 38-millimeter) diameter holes in in a log, and stuff them with suet. Insert a cup book at one end and hang the log. You can also coat a pine cone in suet and hang it up.

MATERIALS ¾-inch (20-millimeter) board for all parts.

ASSEMBLY Place the can and side supports on the back, and mark the position of the supports as shown. Drill holes and attach the supports by screwing the four long screws through the back into them. Nail on the brace. Fit the can in position, and make pilot holes for the two small screws. Turn the screws until they hold the can in place.

SCRAP BASKET

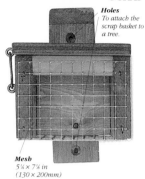

Holes
To attach the scrap basket to a tree.

Mesh
5¼ × 7¾ in
(130 × 200mm)

Kitchen leftovers (see pages 26–27) or nuts are appreciated by many different birds. The simplest container is a mesh bag, but this soon becomes messy. It is quite easy to make a refillable basket to keep food dry. Use galvanized or plastic-coated mesh to cover the front and base of the basket – a smaller mesh should be used for food such as nuts. Avoid sharp edges, and never use collapsible mesh that can trap a bird's leg.

MATERIALS ¾-inch (20-millimeter) board for the sides, back, brace, and batten, and ½-inch (12-millimeter) plywood for the lid.

ASSEMBLY Nail the sides to the back and to the front brace. Attach the hinge to the lid and one side with the brass screws, and fix the hook and eye to secure the lid on the other side. Bend the mesh and attach it to the sides and back with staples. Drill two holes in the batten, and fix it to the back with the longer screws.

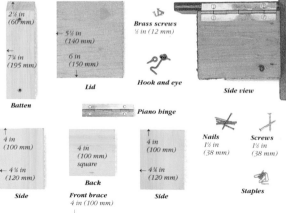

Batten
2½ in (60 mm)
7¾ in (195 mm)

Lid
5½ in (140 mm)
6 in (150 mm)

Brass screws
½ in (12 mm)

Hook and eye

Side view

Piano hinge

Side
4 in (100 mm)
4¾ in (120 mm)

Back
4 in (100 mm) square

Front brace
4 in (100 mm)
¾ in (20 mm)

Side
4 in (100 mm)
4¾ in (120 mm)

Nails
1½ in (38 mm)

Screws
1½ in (38 mm)

Staples

SEED HOPPER

A hopper is the most practical way of providing seed, as it keeps the food dry and prevents it from being blown away by the wind. Other methods tend to be wasteful, although ground-feeding birds prefer their seed scattered on the lawn. This hopper design is simple to make. You can adjust the distance between the mouth of the jar and the tray to regulate the flow of different sizes of seed. To replenish the hopper, fill the jar with seed, invert it while holding a piece of cardboard over the open end, place it back in the hopper, and remove the cardboard. The dimensions given here are for a hopper that will hold a 16-ounce (450-gram) jelly jar.

Hold firm *The webbing allows the jar to be removed and refilled, and the pegs hold it steady.*

MATERIALS 1-inch (25-millimeter) board for the base, ¾-inch (20-millimeter) square wood for the edges, and ½-inch (12-millimeter) plywood for the back.

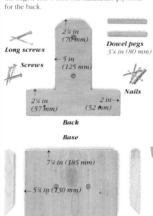

Long screws

2¾ in (70 mm)

Dowel pegs
3¼ in (80 mm)

Screws

5 in (125 mm)

Nails

2¼ in (57 mm)   2 in (52 mm)

Back

Base

Jelly jar

Adjustable flow *Screw the three screws further in to restrict the flow of smaller seed.*

7¼ in (185 mm)

5¼ in (130 mm)

Edges (Corners cut at 45°)

Webbing and tacks
12 in (300 mm)

ASSEMBLY Fix the back onto the base using the long screws. Nail the edges to the base, leaving gaps between the mitered corners for drainage. Drill two holes in the base, and wedge the dowel pegs into them. Screw the three small screws partially into the base, where the rim of the jar will rest on them. Secure the webbing to the back with the tacks.

BOWL FEEDER

There are many seed feeder models on the market. If you buy a plastic feeder, make sure that it is made from a tough plastic, such as Lexan, which is unbreakable and resistant to chewing by predators. The design shown here is a very successful pattern of feeder, popular with a variety of birds.

The height of the dome above the bowl of the feeder is adjustable; if you want to keep large birds out, simply lower the dome until the gap is too narrow for them to reach the food. The dome also acts as a squirrel guard and can be bought separately to protect other kinds of feeders.

Keeping stock *Consider the size and design of the seed container when buying this type of feeder. A bowl that holds a large amount of seed will not need to be refilled too often. The feeder should be easy to clean and fill, and clear plastic will allow you to see when a refill is necessary.*

Easy access *Birds that cling easily, such as chickadees, nuthatches, and finches, can use the perches to reach the seed that is dispensed to the ports below the feeder bowl. Larger, less agile seed-eating birds, such as cardinals and grosbeaks, land on top of the seed hopper.*

TUBE SEED FEEDER

Tube feeders have become extremely popular in recent years, because they are an efficient way of dispensing seed, and the food is protected both from the weather and from unwanted visitors. A favorite with songbirds, these feeders attract the smaller birds, such as finches, siskins, chickadees, and nuthatches.

To appeal to a range of birds, fill the feeder with a seed mix or a variety of seed types in layers. Staggered perches allow several birds to feed at once, although the seed must be constantly topped up to get the full benefits of this. Cardinals searching for sunflower seed may pull out and discard other types of seed. It can be worth putting out a separate feeder for sunflower seed alone to prevent the feeder from being emptied in this way.

Tube feeders are available with different kinds of ports. The size of the holes in the ports affects the kind of seed that can be used in the feeder: a feeder designed to be filled with thistle seed will have smaller holes than one designed for sunflower seed, to prevent spilling and waste. There are also different kinds of perches. Look for a design like this one, with metal perches and ports with reinforced edges that cannot be enlarged by squirrels chewing them.

Some tube feeder designs include trays below the perches to catch seed dropped by the feeding birds, but these can provide landing platforms for acrobatic squirrels, if the feeder is close to trees. Birds that do not fly up to feeders, such as meadowlarks, California quail, and pheasants, may also be attracted to seed dropped on the ground by birds feeding above.

Most tube feeders can be hung or mounted on a post and fitted with a domed guard above or a baffle below if squirrels or other predators are a problem.

Another kind of seed feeder is the red mesh bag filled with thistle seed. This attracts finches, especially goldfinches, which cling to the mesh. This is a less expensive option but is less convenient and more limited in its appeal.

Squirrel resistant *Metal-reinforced holes and perches limit the damage that can be caused by sharp-toothed squirrels.*

22

ANTI-SQUIRREL DEVICES

In many areas, feeders are visited by
squirrels, raccoons, opossums, and skunks.
Although some people like to see these
animals in the yard, they not only eat all
the food, but also chew the feeders.

A problem with squirrels is that they are
extremely acrobatic and resourceful. The
most important factor is the positioning of
the feeder: it should be at least 10 feet (3
meters) from any branch or building. Post-
mounted feeders – on a metal post at least
5 feet (1.5 meters) high – are more squirrel-
resistant than are hanging feeders.

Baffles, or squirrel guards, can be used.
If you have hanging feeders, fix a baffle
onto the line that holds the feeder. This
should prevent squirrels from finding a
footing, but it is often ineffective.
Baffles can be fixed around the post
supporting a feeder. They provide a
barrier against squirrels attempting to
climb up to the food.

Overheads *A plastic or metal roof fixed over a
hanging feeder will protect the food from both
rain and squirrels.*

**Tantalizing
barrier** *A cage
surround to a feeder,
with holes that only
allow in small birds,
can be effective.*

Baffles can be bought or made from
galvanized iron or aluminum sheets. You
can construct a cone to fit around a post or
line with the open end downward. Empty
containers, large coffee cans, or the lids of
trash cans will also work as barriers. All
surfaces should be slippery and should
offer no projections for the squirrels to grip.

An alternative method is to suspend your
feeder from a clothesline or wire, and string
empty thread or photographic film spools
onto the line. These will spin, dislodging
any squirrel trying to cling to the line. Old
records threaded alternately with 3-inch (8-
centimeter) lengths of hose can also be
threaded onto the line as a form of baffle.

**Slippery
slope** *This metal
disk on a spring
tilts when weight is
placed on it,
dislodging any
squirrel that tries
to land on it or
cling to it.*

FEEDERS

· FEEDER FARE ·

SOME BIRDS ARE GLUTTONS and will eat anything that you put out, while others can be quite fussy eaters. Some may be difficult, or even impossible, to attract to your feeder, although unusual birds will sometimes appear, especially in severe weather. A variety of foods will attract a wide range of birds to your feeder, and you can dissuade starlings or doves by witholding their favorite foods.

GRAIN AND SEED

Grain and seed provide fats, carbohydrates, oils, minerals, and vitamins. Some birds eat almost any seed, but most are more choosy. It is not possible to predict any bird's taste completely, although sunflower seed is the most popular with the majority. You have to experiment to find what your birds like. Many stores sell seed mixes for wild birds.

You can also make up your own mix or add seed from wild plants in your area to a commercial mix. Serve seeds in a hopper, with a tray under it so that ground-feeding birds can clear up spilled seed.

Seed in hull

Black-oil type hearts

Sunflower seed
This can be bought in the striped hulls or as dehulled hearts. Hearts are more popular, and have the added advantage that there are no hulls to clear up. The most preferred is the black-oil type.

Sunflower head

Debulled hearts

Cracked corn
This is useful as a source of oil and starch. It can be used to distract large, ground-feeding birds from more expensive seed.

White millet seed
A grass seed with a high starch content, this is a good source of vitamins and minerals. It is especially enjoyed by the small seed-eaters.

Peanuts These have a high fat and protein content, and attract titmice, chickadees, nuthatches, and starlings. You will see birds caching the nuts. Thread peanuts in their shells onto a length of thin wire or string, or fill a mesh bag with kernels. Use only raw kernels, never the roasted, salted types. If you put peanuts out in summer, grate them, because they may be fed to nestlings that could be choked by whole kernels.

Commercial wild bird seed mix
Commercially available mixes contain a wide range of seed and grain. Choose one carefully, or buy a recommended mix.

Canary seed mix You can use birdseed sold for pet birds, to attract smaller birds, although it is expensive.

Thistle seed
This small, oil-rich seed is especially popular with goldfinches.

KITCHEN SCRAPS

Scraps and leftovers from your kitchen are the cheapest foods available for birds. Their use saves the waste of trashing them and cuts down the use of expensive commercial seed mixes. Scraps are often rich in carbohydrates and fats, which help birds build up the vital reserves of body fat necessary for surviving winter nights, for migration, and for nesting. The main problem with putting out scraps is that they tend to attract rats, raccoons, and other unwanted scavengers. Scraps should be placed on platform feeders and in scrap baskets, where these animals cannot reach them or used as ingredients in suet mixtures *(see page 29).*

Crusts and crumbs Bread is a cheap, nutritious food for birds. It is not the best choice, but it helps fill empty stomachs. Brown bread is preferable. All bread should be soaked before it is put out. Stale cake, donuts, and broken pieces of cookies are also good, because they are rich in fat. Fine crumbs will mean that some is left for small, shy species.

Broken cookie

Bread crumbs and crusts

Stale cake

Stale cheese

Stale cheese Cheese that has dried out and become hard is ideal for birds. It makes an excellent addition to suet mixtures, and cheese crumbs sprinkled under bushes are appreciated by shy birds. Mild American cheese is more popular than strongly flavored or blue types.

Donut

26

Baked potato with skin

Starchy foods Leftovers of cooked rice and pasta, and any raw or cooked pastry that remains from your baking, are all rich in starch. They are useful for keeping the most voracious birds busy. Potatoes are also a good source of starch. They last well if they have been cooked in their skins because the birds can carry the soft contents only a beakful at a time.

Uncooked pastry dough

Cooked spaghetti

Cooked rice

Fat and meat These should only be put out in cold weather: in warm weather they quickly become rancid. Put suet, bacon rinds, or fat trimmed from meat into a scrap basket *(see page 19)*. Fat or suet can also be melted over a low heat and poured over branches or pine cones or into a log-feeder *(see page 18)*. Hang up cooked meat or bones, making sure that they are out of the reach of pets and scavengers. Leftover hamburger is also popular, but it must be cooked. Cat or dog food is gourmet food for birds: put it on the feeder rather than throwing it away when your pet is not hungry.

Bacon rinds

Catfood

Cooking fat

Meat bone

Marrow bone

FRUIT

Windfall fruit attracts birds as well as insects, and fruit is an important energy provider in the diets of many birds. Windfalls, and store-bought apples and pears that have passed their prime, can be put out on the lawn or impaled on spikes on the feeder during cold spells. Halved oranges attract northern orioles, tanagers, and rose-breasted grosbeaks, especially in summer. Grapes and bananas will also be appreciated. Dried fruit can be used in suet mixtures or put on the feeder after soaking.

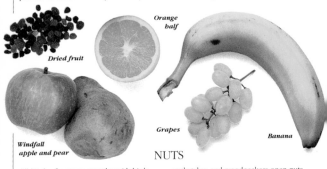

Dried fruit

Orange half

Windfall apple and pear

Grapes

Banana

NUTS

All kinds of nuts are popular with birds, and their fat and protein content makes them a good food. They are more popular in the south, where birds are familiar with them as wild crops. Nuts disappear quickly from feeders, because they are taken and cached. Most species prefer kernels, but nuthatches and woodpeckers open nuts with shells. Chopped or grated nuts will attract smaller species that cannot eat whole nutmeats. A fresh half coconut, hung upside-down on a wire, will attract chickadees, titmice, and woodpeckers (and squirrels).

Chopped nuts

Filberts

Almonds

Walnuts

Fresh coconut

MAKING FOOD

These easily prepared foods appeal to people who have the time to make special meals for the birds in their yards. Suet mixtures, which are sometimes called bird cakes or bird puddings, are a collection of all sorts of ingredients set in melted fat.

Many people experiment with making up their own recipes for mixtures, and it is an ideal way of using up kitchen scraps: a mixture of peanut butter and baked beans has been found to be very popular with several species.

Suet mixtures Melt enough suet or fat to bind the ingredients together into a thick pudding. Stir the ingredients into the melted fat, pour the mixture into a can or other container, and leave it to cool and set. You can then turn out the solid mixture, and put it in a suet holder or mesh bag, or you can hang the container as it is or put it in a holder (*see page 18*).

Seed mixture

Nut mixture

Shredded suet

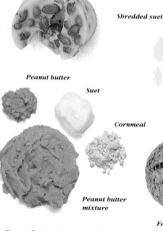

Peanut butter

Suet

Cornmeal

Peanut butter mixture

Fat ball

Peanut butter mixtures The basic mixture is one part fat, one part peanut butter, and six parts cornmeal. You can mix in seeds, nuts, raisins, crumbled stale cheese, crumbled cake or bread, oat groats, or whatever is handy.

Suet stick

29

· FEEDING HUMMINGBIRDS ·

Hummingbirds are the jewels of the yard, whether you are visited by the ruby-throated hummingbird in the east or by one of several species found in the west. All the species are attracted by showy flowers in bright colors, particularly red. Flowers provide hummingbirds with nectar, which is their main food. Protein is obtained from insects: hummingbirds either pick these from flowers or hover around a swarm, darting in repeatedly to seize individual insects.

HUMMINGBIRDS AND FLOWERS

Hummingbirds and the flowers on which they feed operate a mutually beneficial partnership. The flowers have bright coloration, often red, to attract the birds, and copious supplies of nectar to nourish them. The nectar is specially formulated for the birds: it is sweetened with glucose, which hummingbirds prefer, while the nectar of flowers pollinated by insects contains fructose. In return, the hummingbird contributes to the survival of the plant, forming a vital link in the pollination process. While a hummingbird is sipping nectar from a flower, its head or breast is dusted with pollen from the long stamens. The pollen is transferred to the next flower that the bird visits, ensuring pollination and a crop of seeds. The best way to attract hummingbirds to your yard is to plant a variety of flowers that will come into bloom in succession from early spring. Success is most likely if the hummingbirds' attention can be caught when they arrive in spring and are looking for somewhere to settle.

Natural attraction *More than 100 flower species are visited by hummingbirds in North America. The best-known varieties for cultivation are trumpet vine, bee balm, columbine, fuschia, petunia, tiger lily, mimosa, and larkspur.*

30

ARTIFICIAL FEEDING

If you already have hummingbirds in the neighborhood, you can attract them by putting out feeders. Hummingbirds are often territorial, defending their flowers, so you may get more hummingbirds if you hang up several feeders in different parts of the yard.

Hummingbird feeders of various designs can be bought. They can also be improvised from waterbottles used for pet rodents, or even a jar suspended at an angle. Painting the feeder red may help

Hovering at the bar *A broad-billed hummingbird sips from a bottle-type feeder. Initially the red on the glass will have attracted the bird's attention.*

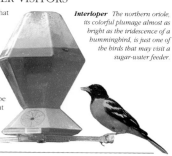

Artificial flowers *One of the many designs of hummingbird feeder available. The four red flower shapes are feeding ports.*

attract hummingbirds. Most commercially available models incorporate red in their design in some way.

Make a sugar solution of one part white sugar to four parts water. Boil the solution briefly to sterilize it and dissolve the sugar crystals. There is no need to add red food coloring. Some people make up honey water, which is more nutritious, but there is a danger of it becoming infected with a mold that is fatal to hummingbirds. In all cases, feeders must be washed every few days with very hot water and kept scrupulously clean.

OTHER VISITORS

Hummingbirds are not the only birds that will come to sugar-water feeders. Orioles, tanagers, warblers, grosbeaks, woodpeckers, and many other birds will visit a feeder if they can perch at it to drink, but they lack the ability to hover.

There are also less attractive visitors to these feeders. While you may be prepared for other birds to share your bounty, bees and ants can be a pest. You can move the feeder so that the bees lose track of it, or fit a bee guard in the form of a plastic screen. Ants can be kept at bay by greasing their approach to the feeder.

Interloper *The northern oriole, its colorful plumage almost as bright as the iridescence of a hummingbird, is just one of the birds that may visit a sugar-water feeder.*

· BIRDBATHS AND PONDS ·

T HE BIRDBATH IS useful in any attempt to attract birds to your yard, because water is as vital to birds as food. It is particularly important for seed- and fruit-eating birds. Birds will come to a birdbath throughout the year, both to drink and to bathe. Bathing helps maintain plumage in good condition and, in summer, keeps birds cool. Water may bring a greater variety of birds into the yard than food, especially in drier areas. Watching the activity at the birdbath is entertaining. Starlings, sparrows, pigeons and doves, warblers, and many other birds are keen bathers.

BIRDBATHS

There is a wide range of birdbaths on the market, but some are more ornamental than practical. From a bird's point of view, there are two major considerations in the design of a birdbath: gently sloping sides to allow small birds to paddle in and out easily, and a rough surface to provide safe footing. Ideally, the bath should also have a deep end, about 3 inches (7.5 centimeters) deep, that is big enough for a large bird to soak itself or for a flock of smaller birds to have a good splash without emptying all the water out. A birdbath with a diameter of about 12 inches (30 centimeters) should be large enough.

Acceptable birdbaths can be improvised from shallow receptacles. The upturned lid of a trash can gives a good sloping surface, but the metal may be too slippery.

Roman bath *Birdbaths can be bought in all kinds of designs, but the features that attract birds have little to do with style.*

Flowerpot bases and large dishes, such as pie plates, are also possibilities. If the shape of the container does not provide both shallow and deep areas, make a submerged island with a large stone. Alternatively, you can mold a simple and presentable birdbath from mortar, as shown opposite.

Site your birdbath near trees or bushes, where the birds can retire to dry and preen in safety. An ornamental birdbath may well look attractive as a feature in the center of the lawn, but it leaves the birds exposed to predators, especially birds of prey.

Improvised *Plant pot bases make ideal baths.*

Birdbaths that are placed near bushes should be raised off the ground – if they are not, it is possible for predators such as cats to creep up on the birds, using the bushes as cover.

Keep an eye on the water in the birdbath, making sure that it is plentiful and clean. It may be necessary to check on it daily in the height of summer. Birdbaths should be emptied out and cleaned regularly, but do not use chemicals – a thorough scrubbing should be sufficient.

Fit to drink? Birds use birdbaths for drinking and bathing, so keep the water clean and free of chemicals.

MAKING A SIMPLE BIRDBATH

Cut a strip of sturdy cardboard, about 3 feet (1 meter) long and 6 inches (16 centimeters) wide. Nail the ends to a wooden block to form a girdle. Embed the girdle in sand, and pour in the mortar mix. As the mortar sets, shape it with a piece of cardboard or metal to form a shallow dish.

A good soak A birdbath should have a deep area to allow larger birds, such as this gray catbird, to immerse themselves in the water.

WATER-DRIPS

One of the best ways to attract birds is to install a water-drip. For running or dripping water, you can buy a miniature fountain or a drip-spout, or you can make a hole in the side of a bucket of water suspended over a birdbath. Put a lid on the bucket to prevent debris from falling into the water.

A lawn sprinkler or a nozzle on a hose that creates a fine spray will also attract birds. Hummingbirds, in particular, like to bathe by flying through a mist. Rather than leaving the water on all the time, which is wasteful if it is not recirculated, turn it on for a while at the same time every day.

Bird lure A water spout is at its most useful during migration. The sound and movement of the water bring in an amazing variety of birds as they pass through.

PONDS

A pond is an attractive alternative to a birdbath, but it must follow the same guidelines to be suitable for birds to use. The edges should shelve away gently so that the bird can wade in. A platform of bricks or stones, or a boggy shore planted with marsh plants, will provide an area of shallow water for small birds.

Simple and effective *A pond need not be elaborate to attract birds: a simple pool, with stones for smaller birds to stand on, is enough.*

There are plenty of books that give technical information on the construction and stocking of ponds. These details are not relevant here – suffice it to say that the simplest way to install a pond is to buy one of specially molded fiberglass, and the cheapest way is to dig a hole and line it with thick plastic sheeting. In either case, you will be left with a heap of excavated

soil that can be piled into a bank behind the pond and planted with waterside plants. You will also find that several birds, such as cliff and barn swallows and phoebes, appreciate water-logged soil as nest-building material.

If you make a larger pond, you will attract birds in other ways. Purple martins and tree swallows, in particular, like to nest near some area of water. Ponds also form an attractive habitat for other wildlife, which in its turn brings in more birds. Small invertebrates and amphibians, for example, are prey for other birds, such as grackles, herons, and egrets. Standing water with plants around it will also become a breeding ground for insects, attracting insect-eating birds that might not otherwise have a reason to visit your yard regularly.

Construction materials *Phoebes will come to the edges of ponds to gather the mud that they use in their nests.*

High-density living *Cliff swallows build large colonies of nests from pellets of mud: a plentiful supply of materials will encourage them to nest.*

Rich pickings *The wildlife that establishes itself in and around a pond will attract larger birds such as grackles, which even hunt in water.*

Hunting ground *Swarms of insects gather over water, providing prey for flycatchers, swallows, and this eastern bluebird.*

WATER IN WINTER

It is important to maintain a supply of water for birds during the winter, both for drinking and for maintenance of the feathers. You sometimes see birds eating snow to get water, but this wastes their energy. To obtain water from ice takes 12 times as much energy as to warm water from freezing point to body heat.

Birds also need to bathe in frosty weather because they must maintain their plumage in peak condition to keep warm. If birds cannot find water, both their flight efficiency and their insulation will be impaired, and this will cost them dearly in wasted energy.

To guarantee the birds access to water, keep the bath free of ice. A bath set just off the ground, such as an upturned trash can lid, may be kept free of ice by a slow-burning nightlight candle placed underneath it. You can rush out with boiling water to melt ice as it forms, but this will be a never-ending job in places where frosts are severe. It is easier to install an electric heater and thermostat, concealed under a pile of gravel. You can also buy a thermostatic immersion heater designed for use in a birdbath. With either of these heaters, be sure to use the appropriate exterior cord and plug, and make sure that the equipment has proper waterproof insulation – if in doubt, consult an electrician. Never use antifreeze or salt to prevent water in a birdbath from freezing, because these will harm the birds.

Expensive drink *This pine siskin will have to use valuable energy to thaw and warm the snow that it is eating.*

· NESTBOXES ·

Nestboxes will encourage the birds that visit you in winter to stay. They will bring more birds into the yard. It is only worth putting up nestboxes if you know that the appropriate birds live nearby: some birds are frequent tenants of nestboxes, others use them only rarely. You can never predict with absolute certainty who will take advantage of a custom-built nest-site. Nestboxes are also used for roosting – groups of brown creepers, for example, cluster in nestboxes on cold nights.

SITING AND MAINTAINING A NESTBOX

The site of the nestbox is of primary importance in attracting birds to use it. The position must be sheltered from the worst effects of the sun and rain and be out of the reach of predators. Baffles fixed around the supporting post or tree trunk, or a wire mesh around the box that allows only small birds through, will keep predators out.

The size and type of the nestbox and its entrance will determine which birds use it, because different species are attracted to boxes of different dimensions *(see page 41)*.

Some birds also like a lining of fresh wood in a box, especially the woodpeckers and others that do not make a nest.

Clean the nestbox out after the fledglings have left, removing old nest material, addled eggs, and dead nestlings. There may be blood-sucking parasites in the old nest, which would attack next year's brood and weaken them. Sprinkling the box with a safe, pyrethrum-based insecticide, such as poultry-dusting powder, is an extra precaution.

BUILDING NESTBOXES

You do not need any carpentry skills to build nestboxes – most birds are not fussy about the appearance of their housing. Some specifications improve the chances of success: neat joints, glued or sealed with silicone, look better and reduce the chance of the nest getting wet in heavy rain. To avoid rusting, you should always use galvanized nails and brass or coated screws, hinges, and catches. If construction is good enough to be watertight, a drain hole in the base of the box is needed.

The plans given here are intended only as a guide. The exact construction depends on your skill, the time that you can devote to carpentry, and the availability of materials. Follow either the U.S. or the metric measurements in the instructions: do not mix the two.

The easiest material to work with is 6-inch floorboard. Thick plywood is effective, but make sure it is of exterior quality. All wood must be treated with a nontoxic wood preservative to prevent it from rotting.

LOG BOX
A natural-looking box can be made from a log with minimal effort. Halve the log, hollow out a chamber in the halves, and drill an entrance hole in one half. Nail the two halves together again, and add a piece of wood for the roof.

ENCLOSED BOX

Small holes, such as the cavities found in old trees, are usually in short supply in the yard. An enclosed box is a good substitute and appeals to a variety of small birds, as well as wood ducks and screech owls.

To hinge the roof, tack on a strip of waterproof material (inner tube or webbing are ideal). If you do not want to inspect the nest, screw the roof down – it is easy to open the box for the annual clean-out. The size of the entrance hole can be crucial in attracting different species (see page 41). Make the hole with an adjustable bit, or drill a circle of holes and join them up with a jigsaw. A metal plate around the hole will prevent predators from enlarging it. A perch below the entrance hole is unnecessary, encourages disturbance by sparrows, and gives predators a foothold.

The same basic design can also be used to make an open-fronted nestbox by cutting a panel that covers half of the front. An open box will be used chiefly by robins and flycatchers and also by kestrels if made much larger.

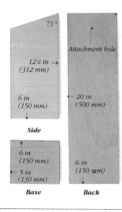

Side
73°
12¼ in → (312 mm)
6 in (150 mm)

Attachment hole
← 20 in → (500 mm)

Back
6 in (150 mm)
6 in (150 mm)

Base
6 in (150 mm)
← 5 in → (130 mm)

Side
6¼ in (160 mm)
10½ in (265 mm)

Beveled to meet the sloped roof

Metal plate
10½ in → (265 mm)

Open front
6 in (150 mm)

Enclosed front

Nails
1½ in (38 mm)

Hooks and eyes

Webbing   Tacks

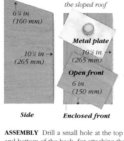

Beveled to butt up to the back
← 8 in → (206 mm)
6¼ in (160 mm)

Roof

ASSEMBLY Drill a small hole at the top and bottom of the back, for attaching the box to a tree or post. Nail the sides to the base, then attach the back and front to these. Attach the roof with webbing or screws. If the roof is hinged, fix hooks and eyes to hold it shut.

PURPLE MARTIN HOUSE

Unlike many other birds, purple martins prefer to nest in close communities. Condominiums for purple martins are the most popular of the nestboxes put up. The key to success is location. There must be plenty of open space, so a field or a large lawn is essential. A nearby pond will attract martins, and overhead wires provide perches. If you feel that you have a good chance of success, instructions on the construction of these multiple residences are given in the pamphlet "Homes for Birds" Conservation Bulletin no. 14, stock no. 024-010-00524-4, which can be obtained from the office of the Superintendent of Documents, U.S. Government Printing Office, Washington, D.C. 20402.

Humble beginnings *A purple martin colony that starts in one purple martin house can grow to a population in the hundreds.*

Put up the box just before the martins are due to arrive in spring. The males appear first and take up occupation, defending their compartments against other martins. Do not be disappointed if the box stays empty: often the house is first discovered later in the summer, by young birds. If these birds survive the winter, they will return to nest the following spring. Once one or two pairs take up residence, you will have a good chance of a colony building up, and more houses may become necessary.

Starlings and house sparrows are a nuisance, because they take over the nest compartments before the martins arrive. You can take the box down or stop up the entrance holes in winter. Put up the box or unplug the holes when the martins appear, and remove the nests of unwanted birds as soon as they are built.

Old-fashioned *American Indians used to put gourds out for purple martins to nest in, and the birds still appreciate this kind of "nestbox."*

OPEN-ENDED BOX

This very simple box has been used successfully for owls, which nest and roost in large cavities. It is wired or nailed to a branch at an angle, to imitate the cavity that forms in the stump of a branch. When you put the nestbox up, spread a thick layer of sawdust or peat in the bottom of the box to absorb the foulings of nestlings.

You may tempt screech owls, and perhaps other birds. The disadvantage of this box is that, being large and open, it needs protection from raccoons and other nest predators.

MATERIALS ½-inch (12-millimeter) plywood for the roof and base, and ¾-inch (20-millimeter) timber for the sides, end, and batten.

Box placement
Nail the batten to the side of a tree branch, so that the box is at an angle of more than 45° to the horizontal. The projecting roof over the opening helps keep the box dry.

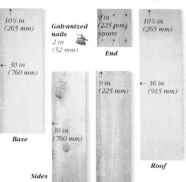

10½ in (265 mm)

← 30 in (760 mm)

Base

Galvanized nails
2 in (52 mm)

9 in (225 mm) square

End

10½ in (265 mm)

← 36 in (915 mm)

Roof

9 in (225 mm)

← 30 in (760 mm)

Sides

Batten
27½ in × 2¾ in
(700 mm × 70 mm)

ASSEMBLY Drill several small drainage holes in the end. Drill three holes in the batten to attach it to the box, and one at each end to fix it to the tree. Hold the batten in position on one of the box sides, mark the three holes on the side, and make pilot holes in these positions with an awl. Nail the sides to the end, then nail the base and the roof to these. Finally, attach the batten to the side of the box with screws, making sure that these do not penetrate the side into the interior of the box.

BIRD SHELF

The bird shelf, which is similar to the open-fronted version of the standard enclosed nestbox *(see page 37)*, provides a solid foundation for the nests of robins, tree swallows, and phoebes. The size and shape of the shelf are not critical, so it is cheap and easy to make.

Nails 1½ in (38 mm)

Long nails

6 in (150 mm)
5¼ in (130 mm)

Mirror plate

Screws ½ in (12 mm)

Roof

Retaining wall *The front wall is just high enough to keep the nest in place.*

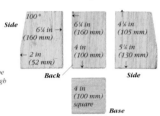

Side
100°
6¼ in (160 mm)
2 in (52 mm)

Back
6¼ in (160 mm)
4 in (100 mm)

Side
4¼ in (105 mm)
5¼ in (130 mm)

Base
4 in (100 mm) square

Front
← 1¼ in (30 mm)

MATERIAL Scraps of timber can be used. For the shelf shown here, ⅝-inch (15-millimeter) plywood was used.

ASSEMBLY Nail the front and the back to the base, then attach the sides. Attach the roof so

that it overhangs the box at the front. Finally, fix the mirror plate to the back with the screws.

BOWL NEST

Cliff swallows build nests of mud beneath gutters or eaves. They usually nest at traditional sites, but you can encourage birds to adopt a new house by putting up artificial nests. Construct nests from plaster-of-paris or quick-drying cement, using a 5-inch (12.5-centimeter) diameter beach ball as a mold. If you leave the bowl open at the top, it will attract barn swallows.

CONSTRUCTION Chalk the outline of the nest on the ball, marking out an entrance hole 2½ inches (60 millimeters) across and 1 inch (25 millimeters) deep. Mold the wet material over the ball to a thickness of ⅜ inches (9 millimeters), and embed a bracket in each side. Nail two boards together to form a simple, right-angled support. When the bowl is dry screw the two brackets into the support.

Molding the nest *Smooth the material with an old, flat knife as it dries. When it is dry, file the edges to fit the frame neatly.*

Bracket *Set brass right-angled brackets into the material.*

Options *The top may be closed or left open.*

DIMENSIONS GUIDE

The measurements are internal, so add the thickness of the boards as necessary. With enclosed boxes, the diameter of the entrance is crucial for keeping house sparrows and starlings out. Even the largest birds need entrance holes small enough keep out cats and raccoons. Allow 2 inches (5 centimeters) between the entrance hole and the roof.

ENCLOSED NESTBOXES

	Floor area	Entrance hole	Height to hole	Comments
Chickadee	4 × 4 in 100 × 100 mm	1¼ in 30 mm	7 in 180 m	Line with woodchips
Titmouse	4 × 4 in 100 × 100 mm	1¼ in 33 mm	7 in 180 mm	Line with woodchips
Nuthatch	4 × 4 in 100 × 100 mm	1¼ in 35 mm	7 in 180 mm	Line with woodchips
House wren	4 × 4 in 100 × 100 mm	1¼ in 30 mm	7 in 180 mm	
Bluebird	4 × 4 in 100 × 100 mm	1½ in 38 mm	8 in 205 mm	Place near the ground
Tree swallow	5 × 5 in 130 × 130 mm	1½ in 38 mm	5 in 130 mm	
Downy woodpecker	4 × 4 in 100 × 100 mm	1¼ in 35 mm	7 in 180 mm	Line with woodchips
Hairy and red-headed woodpeckers	6 × 6 in 150 × 150 mm	2 in 52 mm	10 in 255 mm	Place 12–20 ft (4–6 m) up, and line with woodchips
Northern flicker	7 × 7 in 180 × 180 mm	2½ in 64 mm	15 in 382 mm	Line with woodchips

OPEN-FRONTED NESTBOXES AND BIRD SHELVES

	Floor area	Height	Height of front	Comments
Mourning dove (box)	12 × 20 in 300 × 510 mm	12 in 30 mm	6 in 150 mm	
American robin (box)	4 × 4 in 100 × 100 mm	6 in 150 mm	2 in 52 mm	
Blackbird (shelf)	7 × 7 in 180 × 180 mm	7¾ in 200 mm	1 in 26 mm	
Phoebe (shelf)	6 × 6 in 150 × 150 mm	4 in 100 mm	1 in 26 mm	

SPECIAL NESTBOXES

Tree swallow	Bowl nest	
Barn swallow	Open-topped bowl nest, or half coconut shell	Place 10–30 ft (3–9 m) up, and line with woodchips
Screech owl	Open-ended box	Place 10–30 ft (3–9 m) up, and line with woodchips
Kestrel	Open-ended box	

CHAPTER TWO

BIRD PROFILES

Birds can be enjoyed simply for their color, movement, and song, but anyone with a little curiosity wants to know which birds are visiting the yard. Confident identification is essential, for instance, if the Behavior Guide is to prove useful. The directory of profiles is a means of identifying many species that visit yards or parks, and it describes their typical feeding and nesting habits. Guidance is given wherever possible on distinguishing sexes and age groups. It is more interesting to watch birds if you know why they act as they do. For example, it is useful to know that the hairy woodpecker with a red crown that is being chased up a tree by an adult male, with red on the back of its head, is a young male rather than a female, because it explains the intent of the male that is giving chase.

Markings tell us a woodpecker's species, sex, and age.

· WHAT BIRD IS THAT? ·

The purpose of this chapter is to introduce a selection of common birds that may be seen in yards, parks, and city environs, and to describe their habits so that they become familiar. This reference guide is not a substitute for one of the many bird identification guides available, but it will help readers with little experience of birdwatching who want to play host to birds in their yards and learn more about them.

POSITIVE IDENTIFICATION

To identify a bird, you can either use a field guide or ask a birder. Both work only if you observe and note the bird's features carefully. Otherwise the book will present an array of birds almost, but not quite, like the one you saw, and the birder will not be able to match your description with known birds. Note the bird's physical features and details of its voice, flight, posture, how it walks or hops, and where you saw it.

Size, length of wings, tail and bill, and location (fields, woods, near water) identify the type of bird. Once this is known, voice and plumage show the species. It takes time to develop an eye for the significant details. It is easy to remember bold features and then find that they are shared by more than one species, while a tiny but vital detail has been overlooked, and you may find it helpful to make notes or drawings.

THE PARTS OF A BIRD'S BODY

Cap or crown
Bill or beak
Neck or nape
Cheek
Throat
Back
Breast
Wing bar
Wing
Flank
Rump
Tail
Belly
Rear toe
Front toes

Use the names of the parts on this picture when taking notes. Trace over it so that you have an outline on which you can quickly fill in the details of a mystery bird. Note the colors of the plumage, and the

size, shape, and color of the legs and bill. Look at any stripe on the face: does it run through the eye or above it? It is important to judge the size of the bird: compare it with well known birds, or a leaf or a brick.

THE BIRD PROFILE

Seventy-eight North American bird species are presented on the following pages. They are listed in their family groups in the order of the American Ornithological Union classification. It might seem that it would be easier to find them if they were listed in alphabetical order, but common names can vary from place to place. Also, the scientific classification groups bird species according to their natural relationships, from the least to the most evolved species, so you will find birds of similar appearance and behavior grouped together.

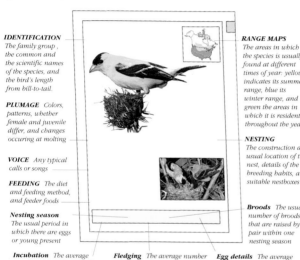

IDENTIFICATION
The family group, the common and the scientific names of the species, and the bird's length from bill-to-tail.

PLUMAGE *Colors, patterns, whether female and juvenile differ, and changes occuring at molting*

VOICE *Any typical calls or songs*

FEEDING *The diet and feeding method, and feeder foods*

Nesting season
The usual period in which there are eggs or young present

Incubation *The average number of days that a bird spends brooding the eggs, and which sex broods*

Fledging *The average number of days until a young bird is fully feathered and able to leave the nest*

RANGE MAPS
The areas in which the species is usually found at different times of year: yellow indicates its summer range, blue its winter range, and green the areas in which it is resident throughout the year

NESTING
The construction and usual location of the nest, details of the breeding habits, and suitable nestboxes

Broods *The usual number of broods that are raised by a pair within one nesting season*

Egg details *The average number of eggs that are laid in one clutch, and their colors and markings*

The figures that are given in the nesting information panel for the nesting season, the numbers of broods and eggs, and the incubation and fledging times, are approximate. They are likely to vary with circumstances. For example, egg-laying tends to start earlier in southern parts of the range, and first-time breeders tend to lay fewer eggs than older, more experienced birds. The availability of food is another important factor influencing the numbers of eggs in a clutch.

Duck family (ANATIDAE)
CANADA GOOSE
Branta canadensis
Length: 25–45 inches (64–114 centimeters)

The legs are far enough forward on the body to make it easy for the bird to walk

THE CANADA GOOSE is the most familiar and widespread of North American waterfowl. Canada geese migrate by day, flying in V-formation. Goslings remain with their parents until the next breeding season. Flocks of Canada geese have become a common sight in city parks and suburban office complexes, and around reservoirs. They have benefited from islands, where they can nest in safety and extensive lawns for grazing.

PLUMAGE The body is dark gray-brown, the head and neck black with white cheeks. The tail is white at its base and black at the tip. There are several races that have similar plumage but that vary in size, such as the mallard-sized cackling Canada goose and the giant Canada goose.

VOICE Canada geese use a large number of calls. The most common is the musical *ah-honk* uttered when flying in formation. Smaller races have higher, cackling calls.

FEEDING "Honkers" eat mainly grasses (sprouting grain crops and lawn grasses), and other vegetation, plus mollusks and crustaceans on shores and estuaries.

NESTING The nest is a large pile of vegetation gathered by the female, usually near water and often close to other Canada geese. After the goslings have hatched, they are led to water by their parents. Sometimes one pair will adopt the goslings of other pairs, so large families may be seen. Canada geese do not start breeding until their third spring. They mate for life, but they will remate if the partner dies.

Communal living *Like many geese, Canada geese live and migrate in flocks.*

Nesting information March through June • 1 brood • 4 to 6 white eggs • 25 to 28 days incubation by the female • 42 days fledging

Duck family (ANATIDAE)

MALLARD

Anas platyrhynchos
Length: 23 inches
(58 centimeters)

ONE OF THE best known of
all birds, the mallard is the
ancestor of almost all domestic
ducks. It is native to western
areas of North America; eastern
populations have been
introduced. Mallards are often
seen on lakes and reservoirs, and
they will come into yards that have
a pond or that are near a lake or river.
Mallards might nest in large yards if there
is plenty of cover. The female could
need your assistance in leading her
ducklings across roads to water.

*Unlike most
other birds, ducks
molt all their flight
feathers at once*

PLUMAGE The male has a bottle-green
head, separated from his brown breast by
a white ring. The female is mottled brown
and black. Both have a patch on the wing,
of brilliant purplish blue edged with black
and white, called the speculum. After
courtship, the male molts into the "eclipse"
plumage, which is similar to the female's
coloring. After breeding season he molts
back into the familiar brilliant coloring.

VOICE Mallards have a variety of quacks.
Loud, harsh quacks come from the female,
and quiet, nasal ones from the male.

FEEDING Mallards eat a wide variety of
animal and plant food. They graze, eat
acorns, and hunt in shallow water for
water snails, insects, frogs, and fish.
Mallards take bread and grain in parks and
yards and can become tame enough to
take food straight from the hand.

NESTING A nest of leaves and grasses,
lined with down, is built under dense
vegetation, sometimes in a tree. The
female, who rears the family alone, covers

Vegetable strainer *Mallards "dabble" for
food, sifting plant fragments out of the water.*

the nest with down when she leaves to
feed. The ducklings leave the nest before
they are a day old. Although their mother
is aggressive towards intruders, many
ducklings are killed by predators.

Nesting information March through July • 1 brood • 8 or 10 white or light green eggs
26 to 30 days incubation by the female • 50 to 60 days fledging

Hawk family (ACCIPITRIDAE)

SHARP-SHINNED HAWK

Accipiter striatus
Length: 10–14 inches (25–36 centimeters)

Wings are short and rounded for maneuverability in woodland

T WO TYPES OF hawk may be seen in cities and suburbs. The accipiters are woodland hawks with short wings and long tails, while the buteos are open-country, soaring hawks with long wings and short tails. Many species are observed during migration, but the "sharpie" is the one most likely to be seen coming into yards to prey on small birds. It darts through trees, across lawns and paths, seizes an unwary bird in its talons, and speeds on.

PLUMAGE Adult birds are blue-gray above, and white cross-barred with reddish brown below, with a narrow white strip on the tip of the tail. Juveniles are brown above and darker underneath. Similar species include Cooper's hawk (*Accipiter cooperii*), which is bigger, with a longer tail, larger head, and a contrasting dark crown, and the red-tailed hawk (*Buteo jamaicensis*), which has a noticeable red tail and frequently perches on utility poles.

VOICE The call is a repeated *kek-kek-kek* when disturbed on the nest.

FEEDING Prey consists mainly of small birds up to the size of pigeons but occasionally includes frogs and lizards, small mammals, and large insects.

NESTING The nest is built of twigs and lined with bark strips and is often sited in a conifer tree. Occasionally an abandoned crow or squirrel nest is used. The parents may strike humans who come too close.

Natural cull *Hawks may prey on birds at feeders, picking off weak and sick individuals.*

Nesting information March through July • 1 brood • 4 or 5 white eggs blotched with brown
34 to 35 days incubation by both parents • 23 to 24 days fledging

Falcon family (FALCONIDAE)

AMERICAN KESTREL

Falco sparverius

Length: 10½ inches (27 centimeters)

Oₙce CALLED THE sparrow hawk, the American kestrel is the most common member of the falcon family in North America. Kestrels are recognized by their hunting methods. They hover, searching for small animals on the ground below, then drop to the grass or fly on and hover again if their search reveals no prey. They prefer to hover when there is a strong breeze to provide lift, and much of their hunting is done from a perch on wires or bare branches.

Often raises and lowers the tail when perched

PLUMAGE The kestrel has a rust-colored back and tail, pointed wings, and white underparts with dark spots. There is a vertical black stripe below the eye. The underparts are more streaked in the female, and the male has blue-gray wings.

VOICE The call is a shrill *klee-klee-klee*.

FEEDING Kestrels eat mainly large insects, rodents, small reptiles, and frogs, but they also take small birds. Surplus food is cached.

NESTING Like all members of the falcon family, the kestrel does not build a nest but uses old woodpecker holes or other

cavities, including niches on buildings. The female incubates the eggs and is called off the nest by the male when he brings her food. Kestrels may come to an open-fronted nestbox *(see page 37)*.

Split family *The male will care for the first brood while the female incubates the second.*

Nesting information *March through May or June • 1 or 2 broods • 4 or 5 white, brown-blotched eggs • 29 to 30 days incubation by the female • 30 to 31 days fledging*

Pheasant family (PHASIANIDAE)

RING-NECKED PHEASANT

Phasianus colchicus

Length: Male 33 inches (84 centimeters)
Female 21 inches (53 centimeters)

T HE RING-NECKED PHEASANT was brought from Asia to
Europe by the Romans, and from Europe to America
in the late nineteenth century. It is now a popular
gamebird. Pheasants enter yards in autumn and
winter, especially in hard weather. The male
usually has a harem of several female birds.

*Tail is carried vertically
when running*

PLUMAGE The male is red-brown above
with brown, black, and white markings
and has an iridescent green or purple head
with red wattles and cheeks, a double
crest and ear tufts, and a white collar. The
female is mottled light and dark brown.

VOICE The cock's song is a loud *KORK-
kok*, accompanied by rapid beating of the
wings. There is a loud *kut-ok, kut-ok* of
alarm. The hen has a variety of calls, one
of which sends her brood into hiding.

FEEDING
Pheasants clamber in
trees for buds and fruit
and scratch on the ground for
a wide range of foods, especially
grain and seeds. Animal food includes
insects, snails, worms, and occasionally
small mammals and lizards. Grass, leaves,
and roots are eaten in winter.
Grain, bread, and kitchen leftovers will
attract pheasants.

NESTING The nest is a shallow
depression under a hedge or in long grass.
The hen pheasant blends into her
surroundings perfectly; as with other
species in which the female is duller in
color than the male, she is wholly
responsible for raising the family. The
chicks leave the nest shortly after hatching.

Nesting information April through July • 1 brood • 10 to 12 olive brown eggs • 23 to 28
days incubation by the female • 12 days fledging

Pheasant family (PHASIANIDAE)

NORTHERN BOBWHITE

Colinus virginianus
Length: 9¾ inches (25 centimeters)

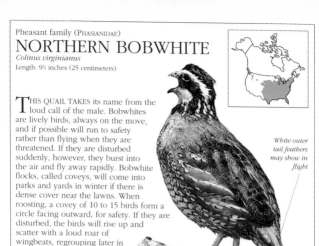

THIS QUAIL TAKES its name from the loud call of the male. Bobwhites are lively birds, always on the move, and if possible will run to safety rather than flying when they are threatened. If they are disturbed suddenly, however, they burst into the air and fly away rapidly. Bobwhite flocks, called coveys, will come into parks and yards in winter if there is dense cover near the lawns. When roosting, a covey of 10 to 15 birds form a circle facing outward, for safety. If they are disturbed, the birds will rise up and scatter with a loud roar of wingbeats, regrouping later in the night.

White outer tail feathers may show in flight

PLUMAGE Bobwhites are a reddish brown, with an eyestripe and throat patch that are white in the male and buff in the female.

Safety in numbers *At night, groups of roosting bobwhites form into circles.*

VOICE The male gives a rising *bob-WHITE*. The most common of the varied calls is a whistled *hoy*.

FEEDING The diet is made up mainly of the seeds of weeds and grasses. These are supplemented with the new leaves of green plants in the spring, with bugs and insects in summer, and with fruit and acorns in autumn. Cracked corn and grain sorghum scattered on the ground attract bobwhites.

NESTING A shallow scrape is dug in undergrowth by either partner. It is lined and domed with grasses and has a small opening in the side.

Nesting information *March through September • 2 broods • 14 to 16 white or cream eggs 23 to 24 days incubation by both parents • 6 to 7 days fledging*

Pheasant family (PHASIANIDAE)

CALIFORNIA QUAIL

Callipepla californica

Length: 9½–11 inches (24–28 centimeters)

Scaly belly helps distinguish it from Gambel's quail

THIS LIVELY BIRD is common in western states, with an introduced population in Utah. Its main home is in scrubby country, where clearings provide plenty of weed seeds, conditions that are often provided in suburbs. The other main requirement of the California quail is water, and the birds are attracted by ponds and birdbaths. Outside the nesting season, California quail live in flocks, or coveys.

PLUMAGE California quail are gray or brownish gray above. The breast is blue-gray, the belly scaly in appearance, and the flanks brownish gray with broad white streaks. The head is dark brown, with a short black plume, and the male has a white eyestripe and a black throat bordered with white.

VOICE The call is a rising *chi-ca-go*, which is used to bring the flock back together after a disturbance.

FEEDING California quail have regular feeding habits, visiting favorite places in the morning and evening. The main foods are leaves, seeds, and fruit, but some insects, spiders, and snails are also eaten. A variety of seeds, from cracked corn to millet, will bring in this quail if there is cover nearby.

Just visiting *Flocks of California quail are often seen in barnyards.*

NESTING The eggs are laid in a grass-lined hollow under a bush, among weeds or beside a log. Yards and roadside verges are commonly used. Female California quail sometimes lay their eggs in the nests other quail, or even of other species, such as roadrunners.

Nesting information *January through October • 1 brood • 12 to 16 cream or buff eggs with brownish gray markings • 21 to 23 days incubation by the female • 10 days fledging*

Plover family (CHARADRIIDAE)

KILLDEER

Charadrius vociferus

Length: 10½ inches (27 centimeters)

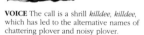

PLOVERS ARE SHOREBIRDS, but many live inland, and the killdeer is found all over North America. Its normal nesting place is in open country, but it will lay eggs on gravel roads and drives, railroad tracks, and graveled and tarred roofs. If chicks hatch on a rooftop, they will jump down and follow their parents to a feeding ground. The black-and-white stripes actually camouflage the birds on the nest. If disturbed, they leave the eggs and draw intruders away, spreading their tails and flapping their wings to make themselves conspicuous.

Long legs are typical of shorebirds

PLUMAGE Brown above and white below, with a reddish rump. There are two black bands on the breast, and one between the eyes. Juveniles have only one breast band.

Start as you mean to go on *Like adult birds, eggs and chicks are almost invisible on pebbles.*

VOICE The call is a shrill *killdee, killdee*, which has led to the alternative names of chattering plover and noisy plover.

FEEDING When feeding, the killdeer runs rapidly forward for several feet, then stops abruptly and scans the ground for insects, spiders, snails, and worms.

NESTING The female makes a shallow scrape in the ground, and her eggs match their surroundings so well that the nest is hard to find. The chicks, which are also well camouflaged, leave the nest soon after hatching but are frequently brooded under their parents to keep them warm.

Nesting information *March through • July 1 brood (occasionally 2) • 4 buff eggs blotched with black and brown • 24 days incubation by both parents • 25 days fledging*

Pigeon family (COLUMBIDAE)

ROCK DOVE

Columba livia
Length: 13 inches (33 centimeters)

T HIS INHABITANT OF
towns and cities is a
descendant of the rock dove
domesticated and bred for the
table centuries ago in Europe. One
variety, often called the homing
pigeon because it can find its way
home over long distances, was used
for carrying messages and is still kept
for racing in competitions. The rock
dove, or domestic pigeon, was brought
to North America in 1606. Native to
coastal cliffs, the pigeon has found the
urban "cliffs" of buildings ideal homes.
Easily procured food allows sick and
injured pigeons to survive much
longer in cities than they would in
natural conditions. As a result, you
often see rock doves with deformed
legs and damaged bills.

*The neck of the
male is usually
thicker than that
of the female*

PLUMAGE The rock dove is very varied in
appearance. The usual coloring is gray-
blue, often marked with white, but it can
range from white to black or brown. The
rump is often white.

Solar heating *Rock doves basking in the sun
are a common sight in city parks.*

VOICE The low, cooing *ooor-ooor* or
o-roo-coo is a familiar sound in cities.

FEEDING Rock doves eat spilled grain,
bread, and any other edible litter.

NESTING The nest of twigs is built by the
female on a ledge or in a hole, with the
assistance of the male. Nestlings are not
fed on solid food until they are ten days
old *(see page 55)*.
Rock doves will use dovecotes.

COURTSHIP The male bows and circles,
puffing out his neck and fanning his tail,
then high-steps with head held erect.

Nesting information Any time of year but mainly March through November • 2 or 3 broods
1 or 2 white eggs • 17 to 18 days incubation by both parents • about 26 days fledging

Pigeon family (COLUMBIDAE)

MOURNING DOVE

Zenaida macroura

Length: 12 inches (30 centimeters)

NAMED FOR THEIR sad cooing, mourning doves are birds of farmland, open woods, and semi-deserts, and they have adapted well to suburban areas. The recent increase in numbers is probably due to the crops of weed seeds on suburban wasteland and food at feeders. Mourning doves nest at almost any time of the year because, like all members of the pigeon family, they feed their young "pigeon's milk," a protein-rich secretion from the throat.

The white edges of the tail show in flight

PLUMAGE The long, tapering tail has white edges. The wings have black spots and are pink below. There is a black spot on the neck. Juveniles have more heavily spotted wings and lack the neck spot.

VOICE The song is a soft *ooh-ah-woo-woo-woo*.

FEEDING The diet is almost entirely seeds. Insects and snails are also eaten, and grit for grinding seeds is important. A common visitor to ground feeders or seed spilled from hanging feeders.

NESTING The nest of twigs is so thin that the eggs can be seen through it. The male

incubates the eggs by day, the female by night. Both parents brood and feed the nestlings.

Good site Cacti are favored nest sites, but trees, such as this palm, and buildings are also used.

Nesting information January through December (April through August in north) • up to 5 broods • 2 white eggs • 14 to 15 days incubation by both parents • 14 to 15 days fledging

Owl family (STRIGIDAE)
EASTERN SCREECH OWL
Otus asio
Length: 8½ inches (22 centimeters)

The ear tufts can be raised or laid flat at will

U NTIL RECENTLY IT was believed
that there was only one species of
screech owl, but ornithologists have
now decided that there are two. The
western screech owl *(Otus kennicottii)* is
very similar to the gray variety of the
eastern species. The screech owl is
common in rural areas but is one of the
most nocturnal owls, more often heard
than seen. You may be able to attract it
by imitating its calls or by making
mouse-like squeaks. The presence of a
roosting owl is often given away when it
is harassed by noisy jays and crows, or
by the pellets of fur and bones that
gather under a favored roost.

PLUMAGE Barred and streaked overall.
There are two varieties: gray, seen mainly
in the north, and red, mainly in the south.

VOICE A quavering whistle that
descends in pitch, and an even-pitched
trill. The western screech owl's calls –
an accelerating series
of whistles and two
trills, one short
followed by one
long – are the most
reliable means of
differentiating
between these two
similar species.

FEEDING Eats
small mammals
and large insects,
but also birds and
other animals.

NESTING The eggs are laid on the
floors of natural tree holes, or in
abandoned woodpecker holes.
The screech owl will use a flicker-sized
nestbox *(see page 41).*

Wide eyed *Although nocturnal, the screech
owl can see quite well in daylight.*

Nesting information *March through July • 1 brood • 5 or 6 white eggs • 26 to 28 days
incubation by the female • 27 to 34 days fledging*

Owl family (STRIGIDAE)

GREAT HORNED OWL

Bubo virginianus
Length: 18–25 inches (46–62 centimeters)

The edges of the wing feathers are softened, for silent flight

T HE GREAT HORNED owl is one of the most powerful and fearless North American birds. Its habitat ranges from the Arctic forests to city parks and suburbs to the Strait of Magellan. As with other owls, the young disperse from their parents' territory at the end of the summer, and this is the time when they are most likely to be seen in built-up areas. The presence of owls is given away by their deep hooting calls and by the flocks of small birds that gather to mob them at their roosts.

PLUMAGE Great horned owls are brown spotted with darker brown above and are barred light and dark below. The ear tufts that give the bird its name are orange, as is the area around the eye, and the throat feathers are white. The great horned owl's color varies regionally, tending to be paler in the south. There is also a very pale Arctic form.

VOICE The call is *whoo! whoo-whoo-whoo! whoo! whoo!* Young owls following their parents on the wing utter blood-curdling hunger screams.

FEEDING Great horned owls usually hunt by night. Their prey consists of other birds, small mammals ranging from shrews to large hares, and occasionally fish.

NESTING The old nests of other large birds are preferred.
Great horned owls may use platforms at least 15 feet (5 meters) from the ground.

Nesting information January through June • 1 brood • 1 to 3 white eggs • 26 to 30 days incubation by both parents • 35 days fledging

Swift family (APODIDAE)

CHIMNEY SWIFT

Chaetura pelagica

Length: 5¼ inches (13 centimeters)

Swifts fly with quick, batlike flutters of the wings

SWIFTS SPEND MORE TIME airborne than any other bird. They feed and mate, gather their nesting material, and even sleep in the air. Because their legs are short and all their toes face forward, they are clumsy on the ground, and usually land on a vertical surface, using the tail as a prop. Chimney swifts are often seen in cities and over yards. Flocks use chimneys for roosting. They gather about an hour before sunset, then descend in a mass.

PLUMAGE Swifts are a sooty gray color overall. The chimney swift is found on the eastern side of the continent. Vaux's swift (*Chaetura vauxi*) and the black swift (*Cypseloides niger*) have more restricted ranges in the west. Vaux's swift is paler underneath, and the black swift is darker and has a slightly forked tail. Swifts look rather like swallows but are more streamlined, with long, slender wings and a short, blunt tail.

VOICE Calls are loud, twittering notes.

FEEDING Swifts feed entirely on the wing. They catch mainly small insects, such as wasps and flies, as well as small spiders floating on gossamer.

NESTING Chimney swifts originally nested inside hollow trees, but they started to nest in chimneys and ventilation shafts as soon as settlers built houses. Lighting fires or starting the central heating in a late cold spell can be fatal to swifts. The nest is a cup of twigs, glued together and fastened to the wall with thick saliva.

Nesting information May through July • 1 brood • 4 or 5 white eggs • 19 to 21 days incubation by both parents • 20 days fledging

Hummingbird family (TROCHILIDAE)

RUBY-THROATED HUMMINGBIRD

Archilochus colubris

Length: 3¾ inches (10 centimeters)

Aᴌᴍᴏꜱᴛ ᴀʟʟ ᴏꜰ ᴛʜᴇ hummingbirds that nest in North America are found in the west. Only one, the ruby-throated hummingbird, lives in the eastern half of the continent, although others sometimes wander up the east coast. The birds' dependence on nectar means that, unless there is a plentiful supply of flowers throughout the year, they have to migrate to Central America for the winter.

Hummingbirds' wings beat up to 80 times per second

PLUMAGE Shimmering green above, whitish underneath. The male has a brilliant red throat patch (called a gorget), a black chin, and green flanks. The juvenile has a speckled throat. A similar species is the black-chinned hummingbird (*Archilochus alexandri*): the male has a black gorget with a violet band, but the female and juvenile forms are similar to those of the ruby-throated hummingbird.

VOICE Hummingbirds squeal when they are chasing each other, and use soft *chew* call notes.

FEEDING Hummingbirds take nectar from a variety of showy flowers and feed on sap oozing from sapsucker holes *(see page 63)*. They also pluck insects and spiders from vegetation. Hummingbirds regularly come to sugar-water dispensers *(see page 31)*.

NESTING The nest is a tiny cup of soft plant material, bound with cobwebs and decorated with lichen and insect cocoons.

Intrepid parent The female, who rears the family alone, will swoop even at large intruders.

Nesting information March through July • 2 or 3 broods • 2 white eggs • 16 days incubation by the female • 20 to 22 days fledging

Hummingbird family (TROCHILIDAE)

ANNA'S HUMMINGBIRD
Calypte anna
Length: 3½–4 inches (9–10 centimeters)

*Recognizable by
the red crown*

A RESIDENT OF THE
Pacific seaboard,
Anna's hummingbird is the
only hummingbird to winter in North
America. It is the first Californian bird to
start nesting: eggs are sometimes laid in late
December. Males have a spectacular courtship
display, plunging at high speed toward a
perched female, then flying away vertically.

PLUMAGE The male is bright metallic
green above and mostly green below, with
an iridescent red crown and gorget. The
female is grayish below with a heavily
spotted throat, which sometimes has a few
red feathers.

VOICE Anna's hummingbird is the only
west coast hummingbird to sing from a
perch. The song is a medley of squeaks
and rasps. The call is a *chit*.

FEEDING Anna's hummingbird feeds
more on insects and spiders than other
North American hummingbirds, but the
diet is largely made up of the nectar of
fuchsia, tobacco plant, and century plant
flowers. A single bird requires the nectar
of about 1,000 blossoms each day. Sap
from sapsucker holes is also taken *(see
page 63)*.
Like all hummingbirds, Anna's
hummingbirds will come to sugar-water
feeeders *(see page 31)* and suitable flowers
planted in the yard.

NESTING A tiny lichen-covered cup is
built by the female in a bush or small tree,
usually in semi-shade near water. The
female may begin to lay her eggs when
the nest is no more than a platform,
adding the walls afterward.

One of the crowd The female resembles other
West Coast hummingbird females, but is larger.

Nesting information December through August • 2 broods • 2 white eggs • 14 to 18 days
incubation by the female • 18 to 21 days fledging

Hummingbird family (TROCHILIDAE)

RUFOUS HUMMINGBIRD

Selasphorus rufus

Length: 3¾ inches (10 centimeters)

Long tongue for probing flowers

THE RUFOUS hummingbird nests farther north than any other hummingbird, traveling up as far as the southern Yukon and Alaska. In spring, the birds follow a low-altitude route up the Pacific coast along the warmer western side of the Rockies. The return to their winter home in Mexico is made by a higher route further inland, along the Rockies and Sierras, where the later-blooming flowers in the mountain meadows provide nectar.

PLUMAGE The male rufous hummingbird has reddish brown upperparts from the base of the crown to the tail, and rust below, with a white breast and a brilliant red gorget. The female is metallic green above and white below, with rust-colored sides. Allen's hummingbird *(Selasphorus sasin)* is similar: the male can usually be distinguished by his green back, but the female is almost indistinguishable from the female rufous hummingbird.

VOICE The call is a soft *chewp, chewp.*

FEEDING The rufous hummingbird is especially attracted to red flowers, such as columbines, penstemons, and tiger lilies. Running tree sap is also taken from sapsucker holes *(see page 63).* Rufous hummingbirds will come to sugar-water dispensers, especially those that have red parts.

NESTING The cup of plant down, moss, and lichen is usually built on a drooping branch of a conifer. Electrical cables and hanging ropes are also used. Rufous hummingbirds sometimes build a new nest on top of the previous year's nest.

Lookalike Females, with some rusty coloring, are identical to female Allen's hummingbirds.

Nesting information May through July • 2 broods • 2 white eggs • 12 to 14 days incubation, usually by the female • 20 days fledging

Kingfisher family (ALCEDINIDAE)

BELTED KINGFISHER

Ceryle alcyon
Length: 13 inches (33 centimeters)

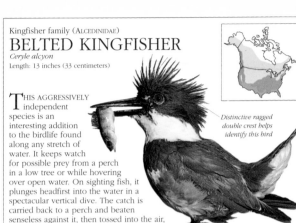

Distinctive ragged double crest helps identify this bird

THIS AGGRESSIVELY independent species is an interesting addition to the birdlife found along any stretch of water. It keeps watch for possible prey from a perch in a low tree or while hovering over open water. On sighting fish, it plunges headfirst into the water in a spectacular vertical dive. The catch is carried back to a perch and beaten senseless against it, then tossed into the air, neatly caught, and swallowed head first. Indigestible parts are cast up as pellets.

Prize pickings *A female with her prey. Belted kingfishers can hover before diving for fish.*

PLUMAGE Both sexes are blue-gray above and white below, with a white collar, a gray band across the breast, and a ragged crest. The female has red flanks and a chestnut band across the belly.

VOICE The call is a loud, rattling *rickety, crick, crick, crick.*

FEEDING The diet is mainly small fish, but includes insects, tadpoles, amphibians, small reptiles, mammals, and birds. Shallow ponds or wetlands with fish will attract kingfishers.

NESTING Both sexes excavate a burrow in a bank of a river or lake or a gravel quarry. It may be some distance from water. The eggs are laid in a chamber at the end of a tunnel.

Nesting information *April through July • 1 brood • 6 or 7 white eggs • 23 to 24 days incubation by female • 23 days fledging*

Woodpecker family (PICIDAE)

YELLOW-BELLIED SAPSUCKER

Sphyrapicus varius
Length: 8–9 inches (20–23 centimeters)

THE YELLOW-BELLIED SAPSUCKER is, in many ways, a typical woodpecker. Its distinction is, as the name suggests, its feeding specialization. While other woodpeckers occasionally take sap from the holes they drill in search of insects, sap is the major food source for the sapsucker. Other birds are attracted to sap left oozing out of bark where sapsuckers have been feeding, as are other animals, including squirrels and insects. There is no evidence that the holes harm the trees.

All forms have the distinctive white wing patch

PLUMAGE Upperparts are barred black-and-white, with a white wing patch and rump. The male has a scarlet forehead and white stripes over the eyes and at the bill. He is yellow below, with a red throat and a black bib. The female is light and dark brown below, with a white throat. Immature birds are brown.

VOICE Calls include a *che-err* of alarm, and a *boih-boih*.

FEEDING Sapsuckers drill holes in soft wood just under bark and lap up the sap with brush-tipped tongues. Insects, fruit and buds, and inner bark are also eaten, and the young are fed sap and insects. Sapsuckers are attracted by nut meats, suet, and fruit.

Feeding sign Over 250 species of tree, shrub, and vine are used in this way by sapsuckers.

NESTING Bothbirds , but principally the male, excavate the nesthole in a tree, and line it with chips of wood.

Nesting information April through June • 1 brood • 5 or 6 white eggs • 12 to 14 days incubation by both parents, the male at night • 25 to 29 days fledging

Woodpecker family (PICIDAE)

DOWNY WOODPECKER

Picoides pubescens
Length: 6¾ inches (17 centimeters)

T HE "DOWNY," the hairy woodpecker *(see opposite)*, and the red-bellied woodpecker *(Melanerpes carolinus)* of the southeast are the most likely of North America's 21 woodpeckers to visit yards and feeders. The downy woodpecker is a confident bird, and you can often see one working through the trees with chickadees. The stiff tail is used as a prop as it works its way up a tree, and the unusual arrangement of the toes – two facing forward and two backward – gives it a good grip when climbing or chiseling the wood in search of insects.

Bristles around the bill protect the nostrils from sawdust

PLUMAGE Both sexes are black above, with a white back and white spots on the wings, and white underneath. The male has a red nape. Juvenile males and some juvenile females have red crowns. The downy is smaller and has a shorter bill than the hairy woodpecker.

VOICE The call is a *chick;* also a horse-like whinny that slurs downward in pitch.

FEEDING The main food is insects found in rotten wood, but large quantities of fruit and tree seeds are eaten in winter. Sunflower seed, corn, cornbread, peanut butter, and suet attract downies.

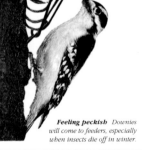

Feeling peckish Downies will come to feeders, especially when insects die off in winter.

NESTING Both sexes excavate a cavity in a tree trunk or branch stump. A few chips are left on the floor as a lining. May use a nestbox *(see page 41).*

Nesting information April through June • 1 brood (2 in southern areas) • 4 or 5 white eggs
12 days incubation by both parents • 21 to 24 days fledging

Woodpecker family (PICIDAE)

HAIRY WOODPECKER

Picoides villosus
Length: 7½ inches (24 centimeters)

*The toes are
specially
adapted for
climbing*

ALTHOUGH IT IS shyer than the similar downy
woodpecker, the hairy woodpecker is the
noisier and more active of the two birds.
From November onward, the male and the female
can both be heard drumming on trees and
posts. This is the start of the long courtship
ritual, which also includes flights in which
the wings are beaten against the flanks to
produce a clapping sound. During
nesting, the male and female change
shifts on the eggs with a short ritual,
one arriving and perching nearby to
call the other from the nest. Once
settled, hairy woodpeckers tend to
remain in one territorial range
throughout their lives.

PLUMAGE Hairy woodpeckers have
white backs, black tails, and black-and-
white wings. The head is striped black-
and-white, with a red nape. The hairy
woodpecker can be distinguished from the
downy woodpecker *(see opposite)* by its
larger size and longer, heavier bill.

VOICE The calls are a loud, sharp *peek!*
and *hueet.* There is also a slurred,
descending, kingfisher-like rattle.

FEEDING The diet consists mainly of
insects, but some fruit is also eaten, and
sap is taken from sapsucker holes *(see
page 63).*
Hairy woodpeckers come to sunflower
seeds, meat scraps, nuts, cheese, apples,
bananas, suet, and peanut butter.

NESTING Both sexes excavate a cavity in
a tree branch.
Will use enclosed boxes *(see page 41).*

Home building *Excavating the nesting cavity
is a task that can take up to three weeks.*

Nesting information March through June • 1 brood (2 in southern areas) • 3 to 6 white eggs
14 days incubation by both parents, the male at night • 28 to 30 days fledging

Woodpecker family (PICIDAE)

NORTHERN FLICKER

Colaptes auratus

Length: 12½ inches (32 centimeters)

The shafts of the feathers show the race of the bird – this is a red-shafted flicker

FLICKERS ARE COMMON across North America, although in Canada and the most northern parts of the United States, they are summer visitors only. The presence of flickers is given away by their ringing calls. Like all woodpeckers, the males drum loudly on trees, utility poles, and houses to advertise their territories. Flickers are easily recognized by their distinctive white rumps, which can be seen as they fly up swiftly from a lawn. Unlike other woodpeckers, they regularly come to the ground to feed on ants, which they pull out of their nests with their long tongues.

PLUMAGE The northern flicker is brown with a white rump, and spotted with black underneath, with a black V-mark on the breast. The male has a red "mustache." There are three races, showing variations in color under the wings and tail. The red-shafted, west of the Rockies, has red, and the gilded flicker, of the southwest, is golden. The yellow-shafted, east of the Rockies, has yellow, with red on the back of the head, and a black mustache.

VOICE The call is a rapid, repeated *wick-wick-wick* and a single *kee-yer*.

FEEDING Flickers feed mostly on insects but also eat seeds and berries. Suet, peanut butter, sunflower seeds, fruit, meat, and bread attract them. Suet holders and hanging logs are preferred.

NESTING The pair excavate a hole in a branch of a dead tree, a large cactus, or a fence post. In suburban areas, they are often driven out by starlings. Flickers will use a nestbox *(see page 41)* fixed to a pole among shrubs.

True colors *A male yellow-shafted flicker fans his tail out in a display.*

Nesting information March through June • 1 brood • 5 to 10 white eggs • 11 to 12 days incubation by both parents, the male at night • 23 days fledging

Tyrant flycatcher family (TYRANNIDAE)

BLACK PHOEBE

Sayornis nigricans

Length: 6¼ inches (16 centimeters)

R ARELY STRAYING FAR from water, the black phoebe lives around reservoirs or marshy areas, or along streams or canals, and is attracted to yards by ponds and other water features. A stealthy hunter, it waits on a low tree branch, often slowly raising and lowering its tail, and then swoops out to snatch insects. The black phoebe's flight is almost silent, but insects are snapped up with a loud click.

This is the only black-breasted flycatcher

PLUMAGE The black phoebe has black upperparts, head, and breast, and a white belly. This pattern makes it similar to a junco *(see page 110)*, but is distinguished by its thin bill and erect posture.

VOICE The call is a short *tsip*, or a longer *chee*. The song is a repeated *ti-wee*, which first rises and then falls.

FEEDING The black phoebe's diet consists mainly of insects, but it has also been known to catch small fish. It often feeds just above water. Indigestible parts of insects are regurgitated as pellets.

NESTING The nest is made of mud and fibrous plants such as mosses. It is built and anchored very strongly on the side of a tree or building, or over a doorway.

Firm foundations *The nest will break before being dislodged from its site.*

> **Nesting information** *March through August • 2 broods • 3 to 6 white eggs, may be heavily blotched with red • 15 to 17 days incubation by the female • 20 to 21 days fledging*

Tyrant flycatcher family (TYRANNIDAE)

EASTERN PHOEBE
Sayornis phoebe
Length: 7 inches (18 centimeters)

BIRDS OF THE tyrant flycatcher family, as the name suggests, hunt flying insects. Eastern phoebes perch upright on a twig, then sally out to snap up a passing insect (often with a loud click of the bill), and return to the perch. The eastern phoebe adapts well to urban life, finding plenty of nest sites in sheltered niches on buildings.

At rest, eastern phoebes bob their tails up and down repeatedly

FEEDING The phoebe feeds mainly on flying insects, from ants, bugs, and flies to dragonflies and wasps. It eats some ground insects and berries in winter.

NESTING Phoebes often nest near water, in tree cavities, on cliffs, and on buildings or bridges. The nest is a cup of moss and mud, lined with feathers and grass. New nests may be built on top of old ones. Phoebes will use a nest shelf *(see page 41)* under eaves or in a porch or deck.

PLUMAGE The eastern phoebe is brownish gray above, and white with a faint olive tinge (yellowish in the fall) underneath. An all-black bill, and the absence of both the wing bars and the eye ring, distinguish it from similar flycatchers. The black phoebe *(see page 67)*, and Say's phoebe *(Sayornis saya)*, which is a uniformly grayish brown, replace the eastern phoebe in western North America.

VOICE The call is a rapid *fee-bee*.

Snapped up *Eastern phoebes often feed above water, hunting insects such as dragonflies.*

Nesting information April through June • 2 or 3 broods • 5 or 6 white eggs • 14 to 17 days incubation by both parents • 15 to 16 days fledging

Tyrant flycatcher family (TYRANNIDAE)

EASTERN KINGBIRD

Tyrannus tyrannus

Length: 8½ inches (22 centimeters)

A S THE SCIENTIFIC name *Tyrannus tyrannus* indicates, the eastern kingbird was the first of the tyrant flycatcher family to be identified and named. It is named for its aggressive nature. Kingbirds will harass harmless birds for no apparent reason. They also fearlessly attack larger birds such as crows and hawks, sometimes landing on their backs to peck at their heads. A kingbird has even been known to attack a slow, low-flying airplane.

Kingbirds fly with quick wingbeats. When hovering, the bird's wings appear to quiver

PLUMAGE The plumage of both male and female adults is slate-gray above, with a white tip to the tail. The head is black. It has an orange crown, although this is not always easy to see. The underparts are white, and the breast has a faint gray color. The juvenile is brownish-gray above with a darker breast.

VOICE The eastern kingbird is a noisy bird, calling often when it is perched, with loud, chattering notes.

FEEDING The diet consists mainly of flying insects. The kingbird has a particular fondness for bees and may nest near wild bee colonies. Insects are usually caught in the air, as the kingbird flies out from a treetop perch, but they may sometimes be taken from the ground or from water. Kingbirds will also pluck berries and seeds from trees and shrubs while hovering.

NESTING Kingbirds usually nest in a tree or shrub, but they may choose a fence post or a rain gutter as a site instead. The nest is a bulky cup of grass and other plant material, lined with fine grasses and roots.

Riverside residence *The eastern kingbird often chooses to build its nest close to water.*

Nesting information *May through July • 1 brood • 3 to 5 white eggs marked with small brown blotches • 12 to 13 days incubation by the female • 13 to 14 days fledging*

Swallow family (HIRUNDINIDAE)

PURPLE MARTIN
Progne subis
Length: 7¾ inches (18 centimeters)

Purple martins often spread their tails in flight

THE ORIGINAL NEST sites of purple martins were cavities in trees and saguaro cacti, old woodpecker holes, and crevices in cliffs, but they have long been accustomed to human habitation. Centuries ago, North American Indians hung up gourds for them to nest in, and today elaborate multiple nestboxes are put out in yards. Purple martins nest in colonies, usually of six or eight pairs but sometimes comprising up to 300 birds.

PLUMAGE The male purple martin is a glossy blue-black overall. The female and juvenile forms are grayish white underneath.

VOICE The song is a loud chirruping.

FEEDING Flocks of purple martins chase flying insects with a typical circling flight, alternating flapping and gliding. Wasps and flying ants are often eaten, as are beetles, flies, and bugs, and occasionally dragonflies and butterflies. Sometimes martins will land and snatch insects from the ground.

NESTING The female gathers mud and sticks for a platform and lines it with straw, feathers, and paper. The male gathers green leaves for inclusion, which may help control parasites.

Nowadays, most purple martin populations on the eastern side of the continent nest in fabricated martin houses *(see page 38)*. They suffer from competition with more aggressive birds that take over the nesting apartments.

Traditionalists *Western populations still use the original nesting grounds.*

Nesting information *March through July • 1 brood • 4 or 5 white eggs • 15 to 16 days incubation by the female • 28 to 31 days fledging*

Swallow family (HIRUNDINIDAE)

TREE SWALLOW

Tachycineta bicolor

Length: 5¾ inches (15 centimeters)

This is the only swallow with clear white underparts

THE TREE SWALLOW is the first of the swallow family to arrive in spring. Other species may be driven back or face starvation if there is a cold snap, but tree swallows can survive on berries and seeds even when there is snow on the ground. The tree swallow is also the only swallow species to overwinter in North America, staying in the southern United States.

The violet-green swallow (*Tachycineta thalassina*) has white around the eyes, and the bank swallow (*Riparia riparia*) has a breast band.

PLUMAGE Dark greenish blue above, becoming more green in fall, and white below. Juveniles are gray-brown above and may have a gray band on the breast.

VOICE The song is a liquid chattering, and the contact note is a repeated *siyip*.

FEEDING During the nesting season, tree swallows feed mainly on insects caught in flight. In winter and early spring, as much as one-third of the diet is berries, such as bayberry and dogwood, and the seeds of sedges, bulrushes, and bayweed.

Fall departure *Like other swallows, tree swallows make their migration flights in flocks.*

NESTING Tree swallows nest near water in tree cavities and old woodpecker holes. The female builds a nest of grasses, lined with feathers. For some reason, white feathers are especially favored. Parent birds will swoop at intruders Tree swallows frequently settle in buildings or use enclosed nestboxes (*see page 41*).

Nesting information *April through June • 1 brood • 4 to 6 white eggs • 13 to 16 days incubation by the female • 16 to 24 days fledging*

Swallow family (HIRUNDINIDAE)

BARN SWALLOW

Hirundo rustica
Length: 6¾ inches (17 centimeters)

T HE BARN SWALLOW is seen as the herald of spring, although the tree swallow *(see page 71)* actually arrives earlier. The barn swallow flies north as the air warms and flying insects appear, and the time of arrival varies from year to year. The first swallows are most likely to be seen over lakes and reservoirs where there are abundant early insects. Swallows are also among the first birds to leave in fall as the insects dwindle. You can see them gathered on utility wires.

Deeply forked tail gives great maneuverability in flight

PLUMAGE Barn swallows are blue-black above and buff underneath, with a red-brown throat. The forked tail has white spots. The juvenile has a shorter tail, and is paler underneath. Other swallows have less forked tails. The bank swallow (*Riparia riparia*) has a white throat and a dark band across the breast.

VOICE The song is a pleasant, quiet twittering. The call is a repeated *swit-swit-swit*.

FEEDING Flying insects are hunted in swoops or circling glides alternating with sharp turns. The swift's flight *(see page 58)* is more direct. If flying insects are scarce, insects are taken from leaves or the ground. Large flies are preferred, but butterflies, moths, and other large insects are also caught. Tiny bugs are hunted in cold weather.

NESTING Buildings and bridges have all but replaced natural sites. Nests are usually grouped in small colonies, and eggs may be laid in neighbors' nests.
Barn swallows may use half a coconut or a bowl fixed to a wall in a shed or barn, or a shelf or nail that gives a foundation.

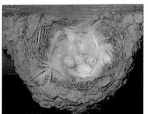

Feathering the nest *A cup of mud and grass, lined with feathers, is built on a ledge or beam.*

Nesting information *April through July • 1 or 2 broods • 4 or 5 white eggs spotted with red 13 to 17 days incubation mainly by the female • 18 to 23 days fledging*

Crow family (CORVIDAE)

STELLER'S JAY
Cyanocitta stelleri
Length: 12 inches (30 centimeters)

Dark foreparts help identify this bird

STELLER'S JAY IS a
permanent resident of the
pine forests of the west. It
interbreeds with the blue jay *(see
page 74)*, where their ranges meet
in the Rockies. It can often be seen
around campsites and parking
lots. In winter it moves into
more open country and
also becomes a regular
visitor to feeders. The
scrub jay *(Aphelocoma
coerulescens)*, another
western jay (with a
separate population in
Florida), may nest in
yards. Farther north, the
gray jay *(Perisoreus
canadensis)* can
become very tame at
forest campsites.

PLUMAGE The crest and the front part of
the body are black, and the rest of the
body is cobalt blue or purplish in color.
The wings and tail are barred with black.

VOICE Calls include a harsh *waah, waah,
shaak, shaak, shaak*, and a mellow *klook,
klook, klook*. The song is similar to that of
a robin, and the scream of a red-tailed
hawk is sometimes imitated.

FEEDING Acorns, pine seeds, insects, and
fruit are eaten, and small birds' nests and
acorn woodpeckers' caches are raided.
Nuts, scraps, and suet attract these jays.

NESTING The nest is of sticks and mud
lined with roots and pine needles. Steller's
jays become very secretive during nesting.

The hand that feeds *At campsites, Steller's
jays can become almost tame around people.*

Nesting information April through July • 1 brood • 3 to 5 pale blue or greenish blue eggs
lightly spotted with brown • 16 days incubation by the female • 18 to 21 days fledging

Crow family (CORVIDAE)

BLUE JAY

Cyanocitta cristata
Length: 11 inches (28 centimeters)

Blue jays' crests can be raised or lowered

QUIET AND UNASSUMING during the nesting season, blue jays form noisy, inquisitive parties from the late summer on. The species is spreading westward, and its success is partly due to its intelligence and the way that it investigates every possible source of food. Blue jays attack cats and other prowlers, but they are not friends of other birds, because they will sometimes also take eggs and young from nests.

PLUMAGE The blue jay is bright blue above and white below. It has a crest and a black "necklace," and black and white on the wings and tail. The scrub jay (*Aphelocoma coerulescens*) of the south is bluish gray above and gray below, with a bluish breast band, and no crest.

Life cycle Uneaten seeds from a buried cache may sprout, helping renew forest areas.

VOICE Common calls are a harsh *jay-jay*, and shrieks when confronting a predator. There are a variety of notes and mimickry of many other species, including hawks.

FEEDING Jays eat almost anything but prefer vegetable food, especially tree seeds, which are often buried for later consumption. Insects are eaten, especially in summer, as well as the eggs and nestlings of other birds.
Peanuts, sunflower seeds, corn, suet, and bread will be taken on the ground or on platform feeders.

NESTING A cup of sticks, broken from branches with the bill, is built in a tree, bush, or vine. It is lined with grasses, moss, and leaves. The parents are aggressive toward intruders, including humans, and dive-bomb them.

Nesting information *March through July • 1 brood • 4 or 5 green or buff eggs, spotted with brown • 17 to 18 days incubation by both parents • 17 to 21 days fledging*

Crow family (CORVIDAE)

BLACK-BILLED MAGPIE
Pica pica
Length: 19 inches (48 centimeters)

WHEN THE LEWIS AND CLARK expedition first encountered this species, the birds were bold enough to steal food from their plates. Normally, however, the magpie is very wary around human habitation. It will often come down to food put out on lawns, but it does not like to feed under trees. This is not surprising because it has often been persecuted as a thief and a nest robber.

Magpies use their feet when feeding

PLUMAGE The black-billed magpie has unmistakable black and white (pied) plumage and a very long tail. There is a greenish gloss to the black feathers. The yellow-billed magpie *(Pica nuttalli)* of central California is identical, except for the color of its bill.

Table manners *A magpie dunks dry bread in water to make it easier to swallow.*

VOICE The calls are a harsh *kyack* or a *shak-shak-shak* of alarm.

FEEDING Like most members of the crow family, the magpie eats almost anything – especially insects, ticks from the backs of large animals, carrion, eggs and nestlings, and some fruit. Meat and bread scraps attract magpies.

NESTING The nest is a substantial structure of sticks and twigs, lined with mud and plant material. It is usually built in a tree or tall shrub, although in some areas magpies nest on buildings or telephone poles. The family stays near the nest for several days after fledging, and the young remain in a loose flock.

Nesting information March through June • 1 or 2 broods • 6 to 8 greenish gray eggs marked with brown • 22 days incubation by the female • 22 to 27 days fledging

Crow family (CORVIDAE)

AMERICAN CROW

Corvus brachyrhynchos
Length: 17½ inches (45 centimeters)

Aلso called the common crow, this is the most widespread member of the crow family. In the south and east, it overlaps with the fish crow *(Corvus ossifragus).* American crows frequent cities, where they feed on garbage, and in some areas they are treated as vermin. Crows are wary, but they come into yards if they are not disturbed, and may become tame. Outside the nesting season, flocks commuting from feeding grounds to roosts are a familiar sight.

Wide, blunt tail distinguishes the crow from the raven

PLUMAGE A large, all-black bird with a fan-shaped tail. The raven *(Corvus corax),* which may at first seem similar, is much larger, with a heavier bill and a wedge-shaped tail.

VOICE The repeated *caw-caw-caw* has many variations. The fish crow has a higher, single or double *cah,* similar to a young American crow's begging call. The northwestern crow *(Corvus caurinus)* has a hoarser and lower-pitched note.

FEEDING Virtually anything edible is taken, including insects, worms, snails, and other invertebrates, carrion, eggs and nestlings, small reptiles, grain, and fruit.

Carrion meal The crow's large, strong bill allows it to eat a wide variety of food, including flesh torn from dead animals.

Crows are attracted to bread, scraps, and corn on the ground and to suet and other food if they can reach feeders.

NESTING Crows are very wary when nesting. The bulky bowl of twigs lined with leaves, moss, and other material is usually hidden in the fork of a tree, but it may sometimes be built on a utility pylon or on the ground. Young crows stay with their parents for up to four years.

Nesting information February through June • 1 brood • 4 to 6 greenish eggs spotted with brown • 16 to 18 days incubation mainly by the female • 28 to 35 days fledging

Titmouse family (PARIDAE)

BLACK-CAPPED CHICKADEE

Parus atricapillus

Length: 5¼ inches (13 centimeters)

A CHEERFUL AND FREQUENT visitor to feeders, the black-capped chickadee is a woodland bird. A woodlot in winter may seem silent and empty, but then a small flock of chickadees will appear, working their way through the trees and keeping in touch with each other by a variety of calls. The acrobatic skills used for finding insects are also employed for clinging to feeders. Seeds are carried away to a perch and held under one foot while they are pecked open.

Flight is fast and agile

PLUMAGE The distinctive black cap and bib contrast with white cheeks. The body is gray-brown above and yellowish below, and the wings and tail are black. White edges to the wing feathers distinguish it from the Carolina chickadee *(Parus carolinensis)*. The boreal chickadee *(Parus hudsonicus)*, which has a brown cap and back, may come south in winter.

VOICE The song is a whistling *fee-bee*, the first note higher. Calls include a soft *tseet*, to keep the flock together, and the familiar *chick-a-dee-dee-dee*, often given by a bird separated from its flock.

FEEDING The diet is mainly small insects found among twigs and foliage. Beetles, caterpillars, insect eggs, aphids, ants, spiders, and snails are popular. In winter, berries and tree seeds are eaten.

Seeds (especially sunflower seeds and peanuts), donuts and bakery scraps, suet, and bones are popular in feeders.

NESTING A hole is excavated in rotten wood, or an old woodpecker hole is filled with leaves, hair, moss, plant down, and feathers. When disturbed, an incubating bird may hiss like a snake.
The chickadee is a frequent user of enclosed nestboxes *(see page 41)*.

Nesting information April through July • 1 brood • 6 to 8 white, brown-spotted eggs • 11 to 13 days incubation by both parents • 14 to 18 days fledging

Titmouse family (PARIDAE)

TUFTED TITMOUSE

Parus bicolor
Length: 6½ inches (17 centimeters)

The crest may not always be raised

WITH ITS POINTED topknot of feathers and large eyes, the tufted titmouse is a very appealing visitor to the yard. The crest is raised when a titmouse is feeling aggressive, for instance when it is about to drive another bird from the feeder. Like the chickadees, to which it is related, the tufted titmouse is a woodland bird that gathers in small flocks during winter.

PLUMAGE The tufted titmouse is a gray bird, paler underneath, with a pointed crest. In southern Texas, it has a black crest. The plain titmouse (*Parus inornatus*) of the southwest is gray-brown and has a smaller crest.

VOICE The song is a whistling *peter-peter-peter*. A high *tseep* keeps the flock in contact and a harsh *jay-jay-jay* is given when disturbed.

FEEDING Titmice feed on small insects, caterpillars, and moth pupae. They also take small snails and spiders. In winter, they eat seeds and fruit, including acorns, sumac, beechnuts, and cherries. Food is often cached.
Seeds (especially sunflower seeds), suet, and bread will be taken from feeders. Titmice prefer hanging feeders.

NESTING A cavity in a tree or an old woodpecker hole is lined with leaves, moss, bark, and hair. Titmice will even pull hair from animals. When a pair raises

two families in a summer, the young of the first brood help feed the second brood. Titmice use nestboxes (see page 41).

Settling in *If tempted into a nestbox, titmice may continue to use it throughout their lives.*

Nesting information *March through May • 1 or 2 broods • 5 or 6 white, brown-spotted eggs 13 to 14 days incubation by the female • 17 to 18 days fledging*

Bushtit family (AEGITHALIDAE)

BUSHTIT

Psaltriparus minimus

Length: 4½ inches (11 centimeters)

Females are born with dark eyes that later turn creamy

THIS TITMOUSE-LIKE bird is resident through the year. For much of the year, bushtits live in noisy, acrobatic flocks, splitting up when courtship starts in January and February. They are most likely to appear in the yard in winter, and they nest where there are shrubs and groves of trees. Bushtits like to bathe, so water is also a great attraction.

PLUMAGE The bushtit is a gray-brown bird with a long tail and a very short bill. It has no prominent markings. The eyes of the males and newly hatched young are dark, while those of the adult females are cream. The males of populations in the southwest have black masks and were once regarded as a separate species, the black-eared bushtit.

VOICE Bushtits utter a high, twittering *tsit-tsit-tsit* as they feed but have no song.

FEEDING Bushtits feed in flocks, moving through trees rather like chickadees, picking insects, spiders, and caterpillars and pupae from foliage. Some seeds and fruit are also eaten.
Bushtits may come to feeders for breadcrumbs, sunflower seeds, and birdseed mixtures.

NESTING The nest is a woven, gourd-shaped pocket, hanging from and supported by twigs, and is usually built in

plain view. Both birds work on the nest, which may take several weeks to complete. It is constructed from twigs, mosses, rootlets, lichens, oak leaves, and flowers, bound together with spider webs. The birds are extremely sensitive during the nesting period. If they are disturbed they will often desert both nest and mate to remate and embark on a new nest and clutch elsewhere.

Front ball A tunnel leads from the entrance hole to the chamber, where the eggs are laid.

Nesting information April through July • 2 broods • 5 to 13 white eggs • 12 days incubation by both parents • 14 to 15 days fledging.

Nuthatch family (SITTIDAE)

WHITE-BREASTED NUTHATCH

Sitta carolinensis
Length: 5¾ inches (15 centimeters)

NUTHATCHES ARE DELIGHTFUL, acrobatic birds that often join flocks of downy woodpeckers and chickadees in winter. Unlike woodpeckers and creepers, nuthatches hop down treetrunks as well as up. They usually feed high in the tree canopy, and their whistled song and repetitive calls can be heard throughout the year.

The beak is long and thin, for probing under bark

PLUMAGE Gray above, with a black cap. The face and underside are white, with rusty red under the tail. In the northeast, the females have a dark gray cap. The red-breasted nuthatch *(Sitta canadensis)* is rust red below and has a black eye stripe.

VOICE The call is a rapid *yank-yank-yank*, the song a series of whistles.

FEEDING Bark and foliage are probed for insects and spiders. From fall, tree seeds are the main food. These are wedged into crevices and hammered open with the bill. Surplus nuts are cached.
Peanuts, sunflower seeds, and suet are popular. Hanging feeders are preferred.

In a flap Clinging to the bark, a nuthatch flaps to deter an intruder from its nesthole.

NESTING A nest of feathers and wool is made in a hole in a tree. Nuthatches only occasionally excavate their own holes. Covering a nestbox with strips of bark makes it more acceptable to nuthatches.

Nesting information *March through June • 1 brood • 7 or 8 white eggs with brown, red, and gray markings • 12 days incubation by both parents • 14 days fledging*

Creeper family (CERTHIIDAE)

BROWN CREEPER

Certhia americana
Length: 5¼ inches (13 centimeters)

On bark, the mottled plumage gives near-perfect camouflage

THE BROWN CREEPER is fittingly named, because it can look like a mouse scuttling up the trunk of a tree. Creepers always climb upward, beginning each journey at the base of a tree, and flying down from the top of it to the base of the next tree. Brown creepers prefer mature trees, where they are often hard to spot until they come around to the side of the trunk and stand out against the background. Sometimes they are seen on utility poles and the sides of houses.

PLUMAGE The brown creeper is mottled brown above and pale below. The stiff tail is used as a prop when climbing. The bill is slender and curves slightly downward.

VOICE The song is a thin, whistling series of notes, the call a faint *see* note.

FEEDING Crevices in bark are probed for small insects and spiders, as well as their eggs and cocoons.
Suet and other fatty food, and occasionally peanut fragments, smeared into crevices, attract brown creepers.

NESTING A nest of twigs, leaves, and moss, lined with feathers, is built under loose bark on a mature tree, or sometimes in a natural tree cavity or an old woodpecker hole.

Favored feeder *Creepers prefer to cling onto feeders vertically, as they do to trees.*

Nesting information March through July • 1 brood • 5 or 6 white, brown-spotted eggs
14 to 15 days incubation by the female • 13 to 14 days fledging

Wren family (TROGLODYTIDAE)

HOUSE WREN

Troglodytes aedon
Length: 4¾ inches (12 centimeters)

The tail is
typically
cocked

IT IS AMAZING that such small birds as
wrens are able to migrate over long
distances, but the house wren and the similar
winter wren *(Troglodytes troglodytes)* travel
hundreds of miles in spring and fall. However,
the larger Carolina wren *(Thryothorus
ludovicianus)* does not migrate. Both male and
female house wrens sometimes have more than one
mate. Males build several nests and try to entice
passing females to enter them, but only a few males
get more than one mate. Once the brood hatches,
some females leave and seek out a second mate.

PLUMAGE Wrens are small, brown birds
with cocked tails. The smaller winter wren
has a shorter tail, a line through the eye,
and barred flanks. The Carolina wren is
paler underneath, with a white throat and
white eyestripe.

VOICE In the medley of bubbling,
whistling notes, the pitch rises and falls.

FEEDING Wrens eat insects, spiders, and
other tiny animals.
Wrens may come to take suet or bread
crumbs from a feeder.

NESTING A ball of grasses, moss, and
other plant material is constructed in any
one of a variety of natural and man-made
cavities. The male builds the nest, and the
female then lines it and carries out all the
nesting duties.
Nestboxes, empty coconut shells and plant
pots are readily used (see page 41).

Single parent *Care of the young may be left to
the male, while the female seeks a second mate.*

> *Nesting information April through July • 2 or 3 broods • 6 to 8 white, brown-speckled eggs
> 13 to 15 days incubation by the female • 12 to 18 days fledging*

Thrush family (MUSCICAPIDAE)

GOLDEN-CROWNED KINGLET

Regulus satrapa
Length: 4 inches (10 centimeters)

THE GOLDEN-CROWNED kinglet shows surprisingly little fear of people. It will come into open cabins and sometimes even allows itself to be stroked or picked up. Like the ruby-crowned kinglet, it has the habit of nervously flicking its wings when hopping from twig to twig. Its habitat is coniferous forests; fluctuations in the populations of golden-crowned kinglets are directly linked to shifts in conifer plantations.

The wings are often flicked as the bird hops around

Winter home *The kinglet nests in coniferous forests, spreading into deciduous areas in fall.*

PLUMAGE Golden-crowned kinglets are olive above and pale buff below, with two whitish wing bars. The distinctive crown is orange in the male and yellow in the female, and bordered with yellow and black.

VOICE The call is three lisping notes. The song, seldom heard outside the northern breeding grounds, sounds similar to the call at the start and ends with louder, harsh, staccato descending notes: *zee, zee, zee, zee, zee, why do you shilly shally?*

FEEDING The diet is almost entirely insects, but tree sap is also drunk. Suet and peanut butter in log or suet feeders may be visited in severe weather.

NESTING The hanging nest is usually built in a conifer, from mosses and lichens lined with soft bark, rootlets, and feathers.

Nesting information *April through July • 2 broods • 5 to 10 cream eggs spotted or blotched with gray or brown • 14 days incubation by the female • 14 to 19 days fledging*

Thrush family (MUSCICAPIDAE)

RUBY-CROWNED KINGLET

Regulus calendula

Length: 4 inches (10 centimeters)

Wings are flicked frequently

THE KINGLETS ARE as small as the largest hummingbirds, and they sometimes hover near foliage while they pick tiny insects from the leaves. This and their habit of flicking their wings as they forage in the trees distinguish them from warblers. Their summer home is in dark, coniferous woods. They are most likely to be seen in yards in winter, when they join flocks of chickadees and other small birds, or when on migration.

PLUMAGE Ruby-crowned kinglets are dull olive above and whitish below, with a white eye ring. It is possible to mistake them for warblers at first glance, because the male's bright red crown patch is not usually visible, being held erect during the courtship display or at other times when the bird is excited.

VOICE The calls are a wrenlike *cack* and a lisping *zhi-dit*, and the song is a varied warble, rendered as *liberty, liberty, liberty.*

FEEDING Insects and spiders are picked from the foliage and twigs of trees while perched or hovering, or they are snatched in flight. Fruit, weed seeds, and tree sap from sapsucker holes *(see page 63)* are also eaten.
Ruby-crowned kinglets will occasionally come to take suet mixtures and chopped nuts from feeders.

NESTING The hanging nest of mosses and lichens lined with soft bark, rootlets, and feathers is usually built in a conifer.

Uncrowned Even if the crown cannot be seen the bird's habit of bobbing its tail is distinctive.

Nesting information May to July • 1 brood • 5 to 11 cream eggs spotted or blotched with gray and brown • 12 days incubation by the female • 12 days fledging

Thrush family (MUSCICAPIDAE)

EASTERN BLUEBIRD
Sialia sialis
Length: 7 inches (18 centimeters)

*Bluebirds can appear round-
shouldered when perched*

THE REAPPEARANCE OF the eastern bluebird in
the northern part of its range is a welcome
sign of spring. Its preferred habitat is one of open
fields with scattered trees, so it has benefited
from the spread of agriculture and settlement.
There has, however, been a general decrease in
both suitable farmland and natural nesting
cavities, and the problem has been made
worse by the usurping of nestholes by
foreign invaders such as starlings and house
sparrows. Nestbox projects have
dramatically reversed the decline of the
bluebird in many places.

Peanut kernels, raisins, and suet are
popular with bluebirds, especially in hard
winter weather.

PLUMAGE The male is a
striking blue above and chestnut
underneath, with a white belly.
The female is grayer above, and
the juvenile is darker above with a
spotted breast. The western bluebird
(*Sialia mexicana*) has a blue throat and
gray belly.

VOICE The call is a rising *churr-wee* or
tru-ally, repeated in the song.

FEEDING The eastern bluebird's main
food is insects, which the bird catches by
dropping to the ground from a post or
utility wire or the limb of a tree. Small
fruits and berries are also eaten, especially
in winter.

NESTING Old woodpecker holes or holes
in dead branches are the natural nest sites.
The duties of building the nest and
defending the nesthole are carried out by
the female. The nest is constructed from
grasses and twigs and lined with grass,
hair, and feathers. The fledged young from
the first brood will sometimes return to
help feed the nestlings of the second
brood.
Bluebirds will use enclosed nestboxes (*see
page 41*). Secluded but open sites are
preferred and precautions must be taken
against competition from sparrows and
starlings and predation by raccoons (*see
page 36*).

Nesting information March through July • 2 broods • 4 or 5 pale blue eggs • 13 to 16 days
incubation by the female • 15 to 20 days fledging

Thrush family (MUSCICAPIDAE)

MOUNTAIN BLUEBIRD

Sialia currucoides
Length: 7 inches (18 centimeters)

Only the belly of this bird lacks the striking turquoise color

THE WARBLING song of the mountain bluebird resembles a robin's caroling and is heard in the early hours of the morning between first light and shortly after sunrise. The future of this bird is a matter of concern to conservationists, like that of the eastern and western bluebirds. Aggressive introduced birds, such as starlings and house sparrows, drive mountain bluebirds out of nest sites, and they are becoming ever rarer.

PLUMAGE The male mountain bluebird is bright turquoise-blue, paler below, with a whitish belly. The female is brown with blue on the wings and tail, lacking the rust-colored breast of the female eastern or western bluebirds *(see page 85)*.

VOICE The calls are a low *chur* and *phew*, and the song is a clear, short warble. The mountain bluebird starts singing before dawn, then stops abruptly when the sun has risen.

FEEDING Through most of the year the mountain bluebird lives on a diet of insects, but this diet is supplemented by fruit when it is in season. Bluebirds are attracted by dried fruit.

NESTING A nest of stems, rootlets, grasses, and pine needles, lined with hair and feathers, is built mostly by the male.

The usual nest site is a natural cavity such as a fissure in a cliff face or an old woodpecker hole in a tree.

Mountain bluebirds use the same nestboxes as eastern bluebirds *(see page 41)*.

Quiet colors *The female, who carries out the nesting duties, is drab compared with the male.*

Nesting information April through July • 2 broods • 4 to 8 pale blue or occasionally white eggs • 14 days incubation by both parents • 12 to 14 days fledging

MOUNTAIN BLUEBIRD

Thrush family (MUSCICAPIDAE)

WOOD THRUSH
Hylocichla mustelina
Length: 7¾ inches (20 centimeters)

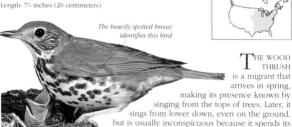

The heavily spotted breast identifies this bird

THE WOOD THRUSH is a migrant that arrives in spring, making its presence known by singing from the tops of trees. Later, it sings from lower down, even on the ground, but is usually inconspicuous because it spends its time in thick undergrowth. It is a welcome addition because its song is, to some people, the most beautiful of any bird's.

PLUMAGE The wood thrush is rich brown above, and reddish on the head, with a white eye ring. The underparts are white with large brown spots. The similar veery (*Catharus fuscescens*) is a more cinnamon color above, with gray flanks and less spotting on the breast. The hermit thrush (*Catharus guttatus*) has a buff breast with inconspicuous spots. Thrashers have longer tails, streaked underparts, and yellow eyes.

VOICE The call is a rapid *pit-pit-pit*. The song is made up of loud, liquid phrases of three to five bell-like notes.

FEEDING Insects and other small animals are plucked from leaves or snatched from the ground. Before migration the wood thrush turns to eating berries.

NESTING The nest is a compact cup of dead leaves and moss, lined with mud and an inner layer of rootlets. White paper or

rags are often used in the outer layer of the nest. It is built by the female in a crotch of a tree or large shrub. The wood

Persistent *The young may continue to beg for almost three weeks after leaving the nest.*

thrush has recently adapted to nesting in gardens and city parks, where dense shrubs have been planted and where there is water nearby.

Nesting information April through July • 2 broods • 3 or 4 blue or blue-green eggs • 13 to 14 days incubation by the female • 12 to 13 days fledging

BIRD PROFILES

WOOD THRUSH

87

Thrush family (MUSCICAPIDAE)

AMERICAN ROBIN
Turdus migratorius
Length: 10 inches (25 centimeters)

Robins have touches of white under the tail, and the outer feathers are tipped with white

THIS IS ONE of the most widespread and best known of North American birds. Populations from Canada, the Great Lakes, and the plains regions of the United States migrate for the winter to join the resident populations farther south. The American robin is famous for its tame, friendly nature, although robins are aggressive toward each other. The robin has adapted well to human settlement and colonized the prairies when they were plowed up. Where its natural nesting places in trees are in short supply, it readily takes to fences and buildings.

PLUMAGE The robin is gray-brown above, darker on the head and tail, and brick-red underneath, with some white under the chin and tail. There is a white ring around the eye. The female is duller, and the juvenile is heavily spotted below.

VOICE The calls include a *tut-tut*, and the song is a loud *cheerily-cheerily*.

FEEDING Robins eat large quantities of fruit – mulberry, sumac, and cherry are popular – and may sometimes become pests, but large quantities of insects, especially plant-eating caterpillars, are also taken. A robin hunting earthworms on the lawn *(see page 15)* is a common sight. Apples, sunflower seeds, and bread will attract robins to feeders.

Shared duties *The male cares for the fledged first brood while the female incubates a second.*

NESTING The cup of mud and grass is built in a crotch of a tree. Similar sites are used on man-made structures. Robins will use a platform placed on a tree or building *(see page 41)*.

Nesting information April through July • 1 to 3 broods • 4 blue eggs • 12 to 14 days incubation by the female • 14 to 16 days fledging

Mimic thrush family (MIMIDAE)

GRAY CATBIRD

Dumetella carolinensis

Length: 8½ inches (22 centimeters)

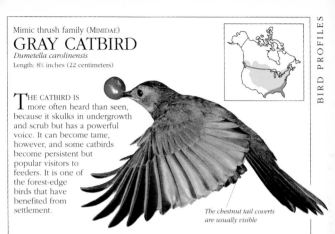

THE CATBIRD IS more often heard than seen, because it skulks in undergrowth and scrub but has a powerful voice. It can become tame, however, and some catbirds become persistent but popular visitors to feeders. It is one of the forest-edge birds that have benefited from settlement.

The chestnut tail coverts are usually visible

PLUMAGE This plain gray bird has a black cap and tail. The long tail is usually cocked up, showing chestnut underneath.

VOICE The call is a nasal, catlike mew, for which the species is named. The song includes mewing notes among a selection of squeaks and more tuneful sounds. The catbird also mimics the songs of a variety of other birds.

FEEDING The catbird's diet is divided between plant and animal food. Insects are eaten in the warmer months, and berries and other fruits are important through the winter months.

Fruit-bearing bushes and vines attract catbirds. Peanuts and peanut butter, chopped fresh fruit, cooked potatoes, suet, cheese, and dried fruit such as raisins will bring them to a feeder. Some individuals even take milk and cornflakes.

Bright berries *Holly, bittersweet, elderberry, and honeysuckle will attract catbirds.*

NESTING The nest is a mass of twigs and leaves lined with skeleton leaves, pine needles, fine rootlets, and bark, and it is placed in dense cover near the ground. Most of the construction is undertaken by the female, with the male bringing material for her to work into the nest.

Nesting information May through August • 1 or 2 broods • 4 glossy, greenish blue eggs
12 to 15 days incubation by the female • 10 to 15 days fledging

Mimic thrush family (MIMIDAE)

NORTHERN MOCKINGBIRD

Mimus polyglottos
Length: 10 inches (25 centimeters)

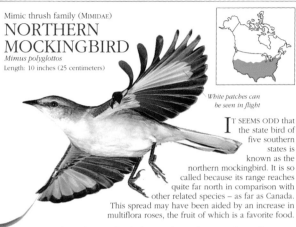

White patches can be seen in flight

I T SEEMS ODD that the state bird of five southern states is known as the northern mockingbird. It is so called because its range reaches quite far north in comparison with other related species – as far as Canada. This spread may have been aided by an increase in multiflora roses, the fruit of which is a favorite food.

PLUMAGE The northern mockingbird is gray with white wing patches, and white edges to the tail, which are seen in flight. Juveniles are light brown with a speckled breast. The similar northern and loggerhead shrikes (*Lanius excubitor* and *Lanius ludovicianus*) show more contrast in their plumage and have a black eye stripe, or mask.

VOICE The call is a sharp *chack* or *chair*. Mockingbirds often sing at night, mostly under a full moon. They imitate other birds, toads croaking, dogs barking, and mechanical sounds such as pianos tinkling.

FEEDING Insects and small animals are hunted on lawns, where the bird's habit of raising its wings may flush out prey. Berries are also important. Raisins, apples, suet, peanut butter, and donuts attract mockingbirds.

NESTING A large cup of twigs, leaves, and grass, lined with rootlets, is built low in a shrub or thicket. Males are sometimes polygamous. Mockingbirds defend their nests by harassing cats, dogs, and people, pecking or flapping at them. No damage is done and the attacks cease after the young have flown.

Berry treasure *Northern mockingbirds are great fruit eaters, especially in winter.*

Nesting information March through August • 2 or 3 broods • 4 or 5 blue or green eggs with red speckles • 12 days incubation by the female • 10 to 12 days fledging

Mimic thrush family (MIMIDAE)

BROWN THRASHER

Toxostoma rufum

Length: 10½–12 inches (27–30 centimeters)

Yellow eyes easily distinguish this thrasher from thrushes

THE BROWN THRASHER'S most preferred natural habitat of thickets and woodland edges often brings it into suburban yards. It forages on the ground, tossing leaves into the air with its bill to expose insects beneath them. Although easily approached, this secretive bird rarely comes into the open, except to sing from the top of a tree. It is not often seen at the feeder.

PLUMAGE The brown thrasher is reddish brown above with two white wing bars, and pale buff to white with heavy dark streaks below. The eyes are yellow in adult birds, and gray to yellowish gray in juveniles. The eyes, the long tail, and the streaked breast distinguish thrashers from the similar wood thrush *(see page 87)*.

Messy eater *Thrashers are named for their habit of flinging leaves up in search of food.*

VOICE Like others in the mockingbird family, the brown thrasher has a varied song, typically repeating the phrases twice. The call is a sharp *smack*. The brown thrasher mimics other birds, but less often than most members of its family.

FEEDING The diet consists mainly of insects and other small animals found among dead leaves. Seeds and fallen fruit are also eaten, and berries of many kinds are important in winter.

The brown thrasher is an occasional visitor for scratch feed, corn, suet, breadcrumbs, and dried fruit scattered on the ground.

NESTING The nest often consists of several "baskets" or layers. It is built out of twigs, leaves, thin bark, and grasses, lined with rootlets, and positioned in a low bush or sometimes on the ground.

Nesting information *March through July • 1 or 2 broods • 3 to 6 pale blue to white eggs, finely spotted with brown • 12 to 14 days incubation by both parents • 9 to 13 days fledging*

Waxwing family (BOMBYCILLIDAE)
CEDAR WAXWING
Bombycilla cedrorum
Length: 7¼ inches (18 centimeters)

The function of the waxy feather tips is not known

T HIS BIRD IS NAMED for the bright red tips of the wing feathers, which look like blobs of old-fashioned sealing wax. Waxwings may descend on a yard to feed on the berries of pyracantha, mountain ash, and cotoneaster. Sometimes they become intoxicated on overripe berries and can be picked up in the hand. Provided that they are not taken by predators, the birds soon recover. Birdbaths are very attractive to waxwings, and in summer they may gather to feed on insects swarming over water.

PLUMAGE Adults are gray-brown above, with red spots on the wings and a yellow tip to the tail, and pale yellow below. The head is brown, with a black eye stripe and pointed crest. The juvenile is streaked. The Bohemian waxwing (*Bombycilla garrulus*) has gray underparts, and white and yellow spots on the wing.

VOICE The call is a high-pitched trill.

FEEDING Waxwings feed mostly on berries, but sometimes they also take maple sap. Insects are caught in summer and are the main food for young nestlings. Waxwings feeding on fruit in the yard may come to raisins or chopped apples.

NESTING Waxwings nest in small colonies wherever there is a good supply of berries. Breeding starts late, so that by

the time the new generation is launched, the berries will be ripe. The nests, constructed from twigs, leaves, moss, and hair, are placed fairly close together in trees and shrubs.
Waxwings will take lengths of wool and string, even from the hand, to weave into their nests.

Get-together *Outside the breeding season, waxwings live in flocks.*

Nesting information June through September • 1 or 2 broods • 3 to 5 gray, black-spotted eggs • 12 to 16 days incubation by the female • 14 to 18 days fledging

Starling family (STURNIDAE)

EUROPEAN STARLING

Sturnus vulgaris

Length: 8½ inches (22 centimeters)

The pale tips of the feathers wear away through the winter and spring

EUROPEAN STARLINGS were released in New York's Central Park in 1890, and they have since spread throughout the continent. They are often unpopular, because they take the food put out for native birds and usurp the nest sites of other birds such as bluebirds. Yet the lively behavior of starlings makes them interesting birds to watch, and there is plenty of action when a flock descends in a yard or park or a pair takes up residence in a nestbox.

PLUMAGE The glossy, black feathers are shot with blue, purple, and green. Pale tips on new feathers in fall give a spangled appearance. By spring much of the spotting is lost, because the tips of the feathers have worn away. The bill is yellow in spring and summer, turning brown in winter.

VOICE The song is a medley of rattles, squeaks, and whistles, especially a rising *phee-oooo*, and often also includes mimickry of other birds and imitations of barking dogs. The calls include an aggressive *chacker-chacker* and a harsh, screaming distress call.

FEEDING Starlings have a varied diet. Their main foods are seed and grain, and earthworms, insects, and other creatures found near grass roots. They stride forward inspecting the ground with rapid thrusts of the bill, which is forced open with each probe.

Bread, scraps, hanging bones, and peanuts will all attract starlings.

NESTING The male builds a nest of grass, sometimes using green leaves, which is lined by the female, in a hole in a tree or a building To collect a meal for nestlings, a starling has to drop one item before probing for the next. Fledglings follow their parents, and are fed on the lawn. Starlings will use large, enclosed nestboxes *(see page 41)*.

Nesting information April through July • 2 or 3 broods • 4 to 6 pale greenish blue eggs
12 days incubation by the female • 21 days fledging

Vireo family (VIREONIDAE)

WHITE-EYED VIREO
Vireo griseus
Length: 5 inches (13 centimeters)

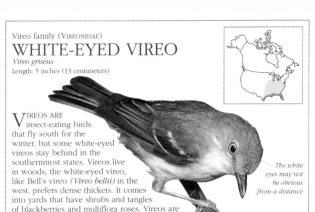

V IREOS ARE insect-eating birds that fly south for the winter, but some white-eyed vireos stay behind in the southernmost states. Vireos live in woods; the white-eyed vireo, like Bell's vireo *(Vireo bellii)* in the west, prefers dense thickets. It comes into yards that have shrubs and tangles of blackberries and multiflora roses. Vireos are active birds: only Hutton's vireo *(Vireo huttoni)*, of the west coast, is sedentary.

The white eyes may not be obvious from a distance

PLUMAGE The white-eyed vireo is gray-green above and white underneath, with green flanks and white wing bars. There are yellow "spectacles" around the eyes. The white eyes can be seen close to.

VOICE The song has five to seven variable notes, which usually include a sharp *chick*. Other birds are also mimicked. The call is a softer, short *tick*.

FEEDING Vireos eat mainly insects, snails, and sometimes small lizards plucked from foliage near the ground. Berries are eaten in the fall.

NESTING The nest is a deep cup of woven fibers, grasses, and rootlets, bound with spider webs, and suspended from slender twigs at the end of a branch. It is lined with fine grasses and decorated on the outside with mosses, lichens, and pieces of paper.

Shared duties *Both parents raise the young, and are fearless around the nest.*

Nesting information *March through July • 1 or 2 broods • 4 white, brown-spotted eggs 12 to 15 days incubation by both parents • 20 to 30 days fledging*

Vireo family (VIREONIDAE)

RED-EYED VIREO
Vireo olivaceus
Length: 6 inches (15 centimeters)

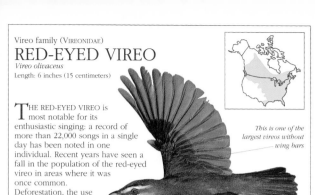

This is one of the largest vireos without wing bars

THE RED-EYED VIREO is most notable for its enthusiastic singing: a record of more than 22,000 songs in a single day has been noted in one individual. Recent years have seen a fall in the population of the red-eyed vireo in areas where it was once common. Deforestation, the use of pesticides, and the increase in nest parasites such as the brown-headed cowbird, which appears to target this bird especially as a host for its eggs, have all played a part in this decline.

PLUMAGE Olive green above, and white below, the red-eyed vireo is distinguished by the markings on its head. The cap is gray edged with black, and there is a white stripe above the eye and a black stripe through it. The red iris may not be visible at a distance, and immature birds have brown eyes. The similar warbling vireo *(Vireo gilvus)* lacks the red eyes and striped head.

VOICE The alarm call is a nasal *tschay!* and the song is varied, some of the characteristic phrases being *cherry-o-wit, cheree, sissy-o-wit,* and *tee-oo.* Red-eyed vireos sometimes sing at night.

FEEDING Red-eyed vireos forage in trees for insects and also eat apples, downy serviceberry, and common sassafras fruit.

NESTING The nest is a thin-walled cup of grasses, rootlets, and bark, bound with spiders' webs and decorated with lichen.

Easy victims *Red-eyed vireos are common cowbird hosts and only rarely reject the eggs.*

Nesting information May through August • 1 or 2 broods • 3 to 5 white eggs, lightly dotted with brown and black • 11 to 14 days incubation by the female • 10 to 12 days fledging

Warbler family (EMBERIZIDAE)

YELLOW WARBLER

Dendroica petechia
Length: 5 inches (13 centimeters)

The wings are spotted with different shades of yellow

MOST YELLOW WARBLERS migrate to Mexico and farther south for the winter, but a few overwinter in southern California and Arizona. They are commonly seen in yards during the migration periods, and they may stay to nest, especially if running water is available. Their cheery song is often heard through the day, and you may see the male perched in a tree, guarding his mate while she feeds below.

PLUMAGE Male yellow warblers are bright yellow, with reddish streaks underneath. Females are paler, with tinges of green. Many other warblers have yellow in their plumage, but none of them is so yellow overall.

VOICE The song is rendered as *sweet-sweet-sweet-I'm-so-sweet*.

FEEDING Although yellow warblers may eat some berries in late summer, their diet is made up almost exclusively of insects. Caterpillars, especially those that defoliate trees and shrubs, are consumed in large numbers, so yellow warblers are useful birds to have in a garden.

NESTING Yellow warblers nest in back yards if there is are dense shrubs. The birds are quite tame when building their nests, so they can be watched at work. The nest is built by the female from plant

fibers, grasses, wool, and moss, and lined with hair and cotton. Yellow warblers are among the birds whose nests are most frequently used by cowbirds for their own eggs.

Self-defense Warblers may build a false floor over cowbird eggs and raise a new clutch.

Nesting information *April through July • 1 brood • 4 or 5 gray-green eggs with spots of brown or olive at the blunt end • 11 days incubation by the female • 9 to 12 days fledging*

Warbler family (EMBERIZIDAE)

YELLOW-BREASTED CHAT

Icteria virens
Length: 7 inches (18 centimeters)

A SECRETIVE AND elusive bird that spends most of its time in undergrowth, the yellow-breasted chat is more likely to be heard than seen. It may sometimes be seen flying awkwardly from bush to bush while singing. Its common name comes from its tendency to chatter, the song being an extraordinary medley of sounds.

The tail is unusually long for a warbler

PLUMAGE As its name suggests, the yellow-breasted chat is a clear yellow on its breast, with a white belly and green upperparts. The head is green with a white stripe and eye ring, and a black area below the eye.

VOICE The song may often be heard at night and includes a wide range of sounds, resembling those of other birds, catcalls, and whistles.

FEEDING The yellow-breasted chat feeds mainly on insects but is also fond of berries in season.
Brambles, hedges, and fruit-bearing shrubs attract yellow-breasted chats.

NESTING The female builds a large cup of dead leaves, grass, and bark, well concealed in dense shrubs or on the

ground. Several pairs may sometimes nest in a loose colony, but the males will still defend their individual territories.

Shy performer *The yellow-breasted chat prefers to remain out of sight in foliage.*

Nesting information April through August • 1 brood • 3 to 6 white or light cream eggs speckled with rust or violet • 8 days incubation by the female • 8 to 11 days fledging

Tanager family (EMBERIZIDAE)

SCARLET TANAGER
Piranga olivacea
Length: 7 inches (18 centimeters)

T HE VISIT OF a scarlet
tanager to your feeder is a
special occasion. This shy
forest bird migrates from South
America for the summer and
usually lives in the treetops. If it
does come into the yard, it is
easily driven away by aggressive
birds such as mockingbirds. Scarlet
tanagers are replaced in the southern
states by the summer tanager *(Piranga
rubra)*, which is less shy and more
likely to become a regular visitor.

*The black wings
distinguish this
bird from other
red birds*

PLUMAGE The male is bright red, with
black wings and tail. The plumage is
molted to yellow-green in the fall, and the
red reappears in spring. The female is
yellow-olive throughout the year. The
summer tanager is red all over, without the
black wings and tail. The northern cardinal

(see page 100), may at first glance
appear similar to the summer tanager
but has a pronounced crest.

VOICE The song is a robin-like *querit,
queer, query, querit, queer*. The female
sometimes sings before egg-laying. The
call is *CHIP-churr*.

FEEDING The scarlet tanager forages for
insects and fruit.
Tanagers occasionally visit feeders for fruit,
and more rarely for suet and bread.

NESTING If scarlet tanagers do breed in
or near your yard, you may see the male
displaying from a low perch. He sings to
entice a female to fly over the spot and
then spreads his wings so that the black
back is shown off to the female overhead.
The shallow nest of grass, twigs, and roots
is built by the male near the end of a
branch, usually at a considerable height.

Harlequin plumage *Male scarlet tanagers
can look very odd during the fall molt.*

Nesting information May through August • 1 brood • 4 pale blue or green eggs with brown
spots • 13 to 14 days incubation by the female • 9 to 11 days fledging

Tanager family (EMBERIZIDAE)

WESTERN TANAGER

Piranga ludoviciana

Length: 7 inches (18 centimeters)

NE OF THE most colorful birds of the Rockies, the western tanager will sometimes appear at elevations as high as 10,000 feet (3,048 meters). A woodland bird, its preferred habitat is conifer forest. It is a quiet bird with a somewhat shrill whistle, but its bright plumage makes it a welcome visitor to yards. It is attracted by the sound of running water.

This is the only tanager with wing bars

PLUMAGE The male's plumage is mainly yellow. The head is red during the breeding season, but this disappears in the fall and winter. The tail, shoulders, and wings are black, and there are two yellow bars on the wings. The female is dull olive-brown above, with yellow and white bars on the wings, and yellow underneath. She resembles a female oriole (*see page 116*) but has a less pointed bill.

VOICE The call is *pit-ic*, sometimes followed by *chert-it*. The song is described as robin-like but is hoarser and lower in pitch than that of a robin.

FEEDING The diet is made up of insects, berries, and other fruit. Buds are occasionally eaten.
Western tanagers will come to feeders for dried fruit or halved oranges and will also take sugar-water from hummingbird feeders with perches.

NESTING The nest of twigs, roots, and moss, lined with hair and rootlets, is built in a fork close to the end of a high branch. Conifers are much preferred as nest sites and deciduous trees used only rarely. The female is reluctant to leave the nest when incubating, even if disturbed.

Staple food Insects hunted in trees and on the ground make up most of the diet.

Nesting information May through July • 1 brood • 3 to 5 pale blue eggs blotched with brown • 13 days incubation by the female • 13 to 15 days fledging

Cardinal family (EMBERIZIDAE)

NORTHERN CARDINAL

Cardinalis cardinalis

Length: 8¾ inches (22 centimeters)

Stout bill for
cracking seeds

N O ONE CAN
miss the
brilliant scarlet of
the male cardinal. If
your yard has berry-
producing shrubs, vines, and trees,
and if there is water for bathing, you
may get a pair of cardinals nesting,
and after nesting, they will bring their
families to the feeder. One of the first
signs of spring is the cardinal's
cheerful song, which may be uttered
by the male or female. At this time, the
males begin to offer food to the
females instead of dominating them at
the feeder.

Drab *Like many females that incubate alone,
the female cardinal is duller than the male.*

PLUMAGE The male is red, with a black
face and a pointed crest. The female is
dull brown with a reddish tinge. The
juvenile male is less red, and the juvenile
female entirely brown.

VOICE The call is a *chink.* The song is a
medley of whistles, such as *what cheer,
whit whit, pretty pretty,* and many other
phrases. The combinations vary, so
cardinals in one area sound different from
those in another.

FEEDING The cardinal's diet includes
fruit, seeds, and many kinds of insects and
small animals.
Cardinals will come to cracked corn, nuts,
and sunflower seeds on the ground or on
platforms.

NESTING The female cardinal builds her
nest of weeds, grasses, and twigs in dense
shrubs and vines. She incubates the eggs,
and the male cares for the first brood of
nestlings while she lays and incubates a
second clutch.

Nesting information *March through August • 2 or 3 broods • 3 or 4 gray to greenish eggs
with brown or purple marks • 12 to 13 days incubation by the female • 10 to 11 days fledging*

Cardinal family (EMBERIZIDAE)

ROSE-BREASTED GROSBEAK

Pheucticus ludovicianus
Length: 7½ inches (18-21 centimeters)

GROSBEAKS USE THEIR bills for cracking all kinds of seeds, even cherry pits. They also descend upon cherry blossoms, pecking out the developing seeds. Rose-breasted grosbeaks frequently feed and nest in yards and parks, but they often go unnoticed because they live in the treetops. The attractive song resembles that of a robin. The similar black-headed grosbeak *(Pheucticus melanocephalus)* replaces the rose-breasted grosbeak in the west, and the two sometimes interbreed where they overlap on the Great Plains.

Rosy underwings show in flight

PLUMAGE The male is black above, with white patches on the wings, and very white underparts, with a black throat. There is a triangle of rose red on the breast, and rosy underwings. The female is a dark buff above, with two broad white wing bars, and streaked below, with pale yellow underwings.

VOICE The courtship song of the male is a long, liquid carol. The female's song is similar, but softer and shorter. The male sings even while on the nest.

FEEDING Seeds, blossoms, buds, insects and bugs are preferred, and some fruit and grain are taken. Grosbeaks will come to a platform feeder for sunflower seeds.

Smartening up *The young males lack the well-defined coloring of the adults.*

NESTING An insubstantial nest of loosely woven sticks, twigs, and straw, lined with grasses and rootlets, is built in thickets or low trees by both adults.

Nesting information May through July • 1 brood • 3 to 5 greenish blue eggs, speckled and blotched with brown • 12 to 13 days incubation by both parents • 9 to 12 days fledging

BIRD PROFILES

Cardinal family (EMBERIZIDAE)

BLUE GROSBEAK
Guiraca caerulea
Length: 6¾ inches (17 centimeters)

The wing bars help distinguish this from the indigo bunting

THE NATURAL FOREST edge and hedgerow habitat preferred by the blue grosbeak brings it into the suburban yard, where it will nest if there is plenty of cover. After breeding, flocks gather and feed on grain crops before heading south to Central America for the winter. Returning flocks of males arrive ahead of the females in spring to establish territories. Usually a quiet, peaceable bird, a blue grosbeak will defend its nesting territory vigorously against competition.

Home decor *The female may work snake skins, bark, or strips of plastic into the nest.*

PLUMAGE The male is deep blue with two rust-colored wing bars. The blue color is iridescence; the birds appear black in poor light. The female is brown with two rust-colored wing bars.

VOICE The male sings a sweet melodious song, similar to that of a purple finch *(see page 118)* or an indigo bunting *(see opposite)*, from a utility wire or the top of a tree or bush.

FEEDING Insects, weed seeds, and wild fruit are picked from the ground. Seed on the ground attracts these birds.

NESTING Built low in trees, shrubs, or vines, the nest is a cup of grasses, rootlets, weeds, and leaves.

Nesting information May through August • 1 or 2 broods • 2 to 5 light blue eggs • 11 days incubation by the female • 13 days fledging

BLUE GROSBEAK

Cardinal family (EMBERIZIDAE)

INDIGO BUNTING

Passerina cyanea

Length: 5½ inches (14 centimeters)

D URING THEIR MIGRATIONS, small flocks of these birds, sometimes made up of colorful males, invade the yard. If they arrive with evening grosbeaks *(see page 124)*, cardinals *(see page 100)*, and painted buntings *(see page 104)*, you will be treated to a display of color that rivals any flowerbed. Recently some indigo buntings have stopped migrating to South America. Flocks now spend the winter in Florida, and they are increasingly being seen in northern states.

The plumage may appear black in poor light

PLUMAGE The male is deep iridescent blue, appearing black in poor light, with a small black area around the base of the bill. The female and juvenile forms are dull brown, darker on the back and streaked underneath. The similar blue grosbeak *(see opposite)* is larger and has wing bars.

VOICE The call is a sharp *tsick*. The song is a series of double notes that has been described as *sweet-sweet, where-where, here-here, see-it, see-it.* In some areas, it includes elements of the song of the lazuli buntings *(Passerina amoena)*. Indigo buntings sing throughout the day and continue singing into late summer, after other birds have become silent.

FEEDING The indigo bunting eats a variety of insects and seeds, as well as berries in the fall.
Buntings are attracted to peanuts, millet, and seeds.

NESTING Indigo buntings live in low, dense growth such as overgrown orchards, or where vegetation is regularly cut under utility cables, and in dense shrubs. The female builds the nest of grasses, leaves, and hair near the ground.

Absent fathers Male parental care varies, but usually all the work is left to the female.

> *Nesting information* May through August • 2 broods • 3 or 4 bluish white eggs • 12 to 13 days incubation by the female • 8 to 10 days fledging

Cardinal family (EMBERIZIDAE)
PAINTED BUNTING
Passerina ciris
Length: 5½ inches (14 centimeters)

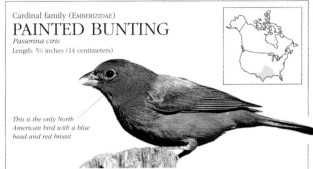

This is the only North American bird with a blue head and red breast

PERHAPS THE MOST COLORFUL of North American birds, the painted bunting is shy and apt to flit off at the first sign of an intrusion. A yard must provide plenty of cover to entice painted buntings into it. Only during the mating season will the male lose this characteristic caution, singing from a perch in the open. In spite of this apparent reticence, painted buntings are formidable fighters: unlike most birds, whose combats are largely bluff, they will fight fiercely, and sometimes to the death, in territorial disputes.

PLUMAGE The male has a green back, reddish wings, and bright red underparts. The head is blue with a red eye ring. Rather than coming from any pigment in the feathers, the blue color is an effect caused by the way that the light is reflected from them, with the result that the head may appear black in poor light. The female is green above and yellowish green below.

VOICE Quiet twittering or chipping notes may be heard, and the male sings a sweet, thin, tinkling song in courtship.

FEEDING The diet consists mainly of seeds, but insects, spiders, and caterpillars are also favored.
Painted buntings will come to feeders for sunflower seed and seed mixes.

NESTING The nest is a cup of grasses, weed stalks, and leaves, usually built low in dense cover.

Verdant bird *The female painted bunting is the most uniformly green small finch.*

Nesting information *March through July • 2 to 4 broods • 3 to 5 pale blue eggs spotted with brown • 11 to 12 days incubation by female • 12 to 14 days fledging*

Sparrow family (EMBERIZIDAE)

RUFOUS-SIDED TOWHEE

Pipilo erythrophthalmus
Length: 8½ inches (22 centimeters)

The white flashes that all forms have on the tail can be seen in flight

The female has the same color pattern as the male but is brown rather than black

T HE RUFOUS-SIDED towhee is a bird of dense undergrowth, more often heard than seen and identified by its distinctive call. Towhees come into yards with bushes and brush piles, and can be heard scratching for food on bare ground under cover. Their usual method of feeding is to rake with their feet to reveal seeds and insects. The towhee's range is gradually extending northwards.

PLUMAGE The male is black above and white below, with a black breast and red sides. The female is brown above, and the juvenile has scaly plumage. All have white patches on the wings and tail. Western birds, once called spotted towhees, have white wing bars and white flecks above.

VOICE Calls are the *to-WHEE* that gives the bird its name, *chee-WINK*, and *jor-eee*. The song is rendered as *DRINK-your-tea*.

FEEDING Beetles, ants, spiders, snails, and other small animals are the main part of the diet. Berries and the seeds of weeds and grasses are also important. Scattered sunflower seed, cracked corn, and peanut kernels will tempt towhees.

NESTING The nest of grasses, rootlets, twigs, and leaves, lined with hair and grass, is built by the female on the ground or sometimes in low shrubs or vines.

Home ground *A towhee nest among young trees on the woodland floor, its natural habitat.*

Nesting information *April through August • 2 broods • 3 or 4 gray or cream eggs with brown speckles • 12 to 13 days incubation by the female • 10 to 12 days fledging*

105

Sparrow family (EMBERIZIDAE)

AMERICAN TREE SPARROW

Spizella arborea
Length: 6 inches (15 centimeters)

The upper part of the bill is dark, the lower part yellow

The characteristic blotch on the breast makes it easy to identify the tree sparrow

ALTHOUGH THE scientific and the common names suggest woods as their home, few birds spend less time in trees than tree sparrows. In winter, they come south in flocks of 30 to 40 birds, which are seen around hedges, fields, and marshes. The breeding grounds are open plains just south of the Arctic tundra, and even here the birds nest on or near the ground.

PLUMAGE The chestnut back has white and black streaks, and the underparts are gray, with a brown blotch on the breast. The head is white with a chestnut cap and streak through the eye.

VOICE Birds in a flock converse in musical *teedle eet, teedle eet* notes. The courtship song of the male is one or two high, sweet notes, followed by warbling.

FEEDING Tree sparrows forage on the ground for weed and grass seeds, which they eat in great numbers. They also eat insects and some fruit.
Wild bird seed mixes will attract tree sparrows, and white millet is also a favorite food.

NESTING The nest is constructed of grasses, moss, and bark, sometimes lined with ptarmigan feathers, hair, and fur. It is built by the female in a tussock or in a shallow depression in the ground.

Winter survivors *Tree sparrows can survive bitter cold as long as they can find food.*

Nesting information May through July • 1 brood • 3 to 6 brown-speckled, pale blue or green eggs • 12 to 13 days incubation by the female • Young leave nest at 10 days, unable to fly

Sparrow family (EMBERIZIDAE)

CHIPPING SPARROW

Spizella passerina

Length: 5–5¾ inches (13–15 centimeters)

The bill is black during breeding, and then turns brown

T HE CHIPPING SPARROW is one of the most familiar sparrows because it is a common yard species, often feeding on lawns and uncultivated ground and nesting in evergreens and shrubs near houses. It is not shy of human presence and with time will learn to take food from the hand. Family groups wander after breeding and before migration, and in winter, small flocks of up to 50 birds forage together.

PLUMAGE Chipping sparrows are light brown or drab streaked with rust-brown above, with a bright chestnut cap. There is a black streak through the eye and a broad white line above it. In winter the cap and the black eye stripe become duller and less noticeable. The underparts are unmarked gray.

VOICE The *chip* call notes and song give this bird its name. The song may sometimes be heard at night.

FEEDING The diet consists of seeds and insects. Chipping sparrows also peck at salt blocks.

The chipping sparrow will come to a variety of seeds and crumbs. Food should be scattered widely on the ground, to reduce competition with other, more aggressive species.

NESTING The female builds a nest of grasses, weeds, and rootlets, lined with hair, in a tree, shrub, or tangled vine, or near the foundation of a building.

Unusual site *This chipping sparrow finds a tangle of game traps a suitable nest foundation.*

Nesting information March through August • 2 broods • 3 to 5 pale blue-green eggs, marked with blue, brown, and black • 11 to 14 days incubation by the female • 8 to 12 days fledging

Sparrow family (EMBERIZIDAE)

SONG SPARROW

Melospiza melodia
Length: 5½–7 inches (14–18 centimeters)

The tail is pumped up and down in flight

T HE SONG SPARROW is one of the best known of the many different North American sparrows, although its plumage lacks the bright patches of color worn by many other sparrows. Found everywhere but the most northern parts of the continent it is a common inhabitant of yards, and makes good use of feeders in the winter and birdbaths throughout the year. The bird's pleasant song may be heard at any time of the year.

PLUMAGE The song sparrow's appearance varies through its range. Generally, it has streaked brown upperparts and is whitish underneath, with dark streaks that meet in a spot in the center of the breast. There is a gray stripe above the eye.

VOICE The song sparrow has 21 different calls and songs. The main call is a nasal *chimp*. The song was rendered by Henry Thoreau as *Maids! Maids! Maids! Hang-up-your-teakettle-ettle-ettle!*, but it is variable enough for some individuals to be recognized by their song.

FEEDING The song sparrow scratches for insects and other small animals and for seeds. It also eats berries. After snowfall, song sparrows scratch away the snow to reveal the fallen seeds.
Sunflower seeds and other seeds, bread crumbs, and millet are taken from platforms or the ground under feeders.

Home lover *Resident birds stay on or near their territory even through severe weather.*

NESTING Nesting starts early, and the first nests of the season are built on the ground, under clumps of grass or thick weeds. Later, when the new leaves of deciduous bushes provide cover, nests are built above the ground in the foliage.

Nesting information *February through August • 2 or 3 broods • 3 to 6 pale green eggs with reddish brown spots • 12 to 13 days incubation by the female • 10 days fledging*

Sparrow family (EMBERIZIDAE)

WHITE-THROATED SPARROW

Zonotrichia albicollis

Length: 6¾ inches (17 centimeters)

MOST WHITE-THROATED sparrows breed in Canada and migrate to the southern United States in the colder months, but increasing numbers are overwintering in the northeastern states. In these areas they have become the most common of the many sparrow species to visit yards and feeders. It is possible that the increasing popularity of feeding birds has helped these "white-throats" survive the hardship of the northern winters.

The breast may be dull or streaked in juveniles

Winter split *As with many other species, the dominant adult males tend to winter farther north than do females and immatures.*

PLUMAGE White-throats have rust-brown upperparts and grayish underparts. The white throat is conspicuous. There are broad black-and-white stripes through the eye and over the crown, and a small patch

of yellow in front of the eye. The juvenile has streaked light and dark underparts and a grayish throat.

VOICE Calls include a *pink* and a *seet*. The whistling song is rendered as *Old Sam Peabody, Peabody, Peabody* or *Pure sweet Canada, Canada, Canada.*

FEEDING The white-throat forages for weed seeds, scratching the ground with each foot in turn. Insects are also eaten. Millet, sunflower seed, and cracked grain and other seeds are taken from the ground or from platforms.

NESTING The nest of twigs and grasses is built by the female. It is usually placed on the ground, well concealed under the cover of a bush or brush pile, but is sometimes built just above the ground in thick vegetation.

Nesting information May through August • 1 brood • 4 to 6 bluish or greenish white eggs with brown speckles • 12 to 14 days incubation by the female • 7 to 12 days fledging

Sparrow family (EMBERIZIDAE)

DARK-EYED JUNCO

Junco hyemalis
Length: 6¼ inches (16 centimeters)

DISTINCTIVE AND POPULAR in yards and at feeders, dark-eyed juncos are birds of forest edges and glades, which makes leafy suburban neighborhoods excellent habitats for them. They breed in Canada and the northern United States and migrate to southern areas for the winter, where they are called snowbirds. Juncos live in flocks, so 20 or more juncos may suddenly appear at a feeder.

White outer tail feathers may be visible in flight

All juncos are pale below

PLUMAGE There are four races of dark-eyed junco, which were once thought of as separate species. All have pink bills and white outer tail feathers, but the males show variations to the color of the upper body. The widespread "slate-colored" junco is dark gray above. The western "Oregon" junco has a black head and neck and brown back and sides, but there is also a "pink-sided" variety in the central Rockies with a gray head and neck and pinkish sides. The "gray-headed" juncos of

the southern Rockies are largely gray, with brown backs, and the "white-winged" juncos found in the Black Hills of South Dakota and Wyoming are pale gray above, with two white wingbars. Females of all races are more brown overall, and juveniles are striped like house sparrows *(see page 125)*.

VOICE The song is a long, jingling trill, and the calls are a pebble-tapping *clink* note and a *tack-tack* when disturbed.

FEEDING Juncos search on the ground for insects in summer and seeds in winter. Juncos sometimes perch on feeders with a ledge but mostly take seeds spilled onto the ground. They appear in yards at the start of winter and depart in spring.

NESTING The female, with the male helping to gather material, builds the nest of grasses, rootlets, and bark on the ground under roots, overhanging banks, and brush piles, or occasionally in bushes.

Variation on a theme *Oregon juncos have the typical dark and light plumage pattern.*

Nesting information April through August • 2 broods • 4 or 5 gray, brown-speckled eggs
11 to 12 days incubation by the female • 12 to 13 days fledging

Blackbird family (EMBERIZIDAE)

BOBOLINK

Dolichonyx oryzivorus
Length: 6 inches (15 centimeters)

T HE STRIKING PLUMAGE OF the male bobolink during its spring migration is so completely different from its appearance on the fall migration that for a long time it was thought that they were two separate birds. During the nineteenth and early twentieth centuries, bobolinks fed in rice fields along the fall migration route. They were called rice birds and were shot by the thousand. So many bobolinks were killed that the population has never fully recovered, although the bird is now protected by law. Currently, hay-mowing in June seriously impairs the breeding success of the species.

The tail has stiff, spiny feathers, like a woodpecker's, and is dragged along the ground in courtship displays

True identity Spring and fall bobolinks were once thought of as two different birds.

PLUMAGE After the summer molt, both sexes are streaked light and dark brown on top and light brown below, with a broad stripe above the eye and a narrow stripe through it. During winter the feather tips wear away, and the male's breeding plumage appears: black-and-white above with a white rump and a yellow nape, and black wings, tail, head, and underparts.

VOICE The call is a metallic *pink*. The song is rendered in various ways including *bobolink, bobolink, spink, spank, spink.*

FEEDING In summer, the diet is insects, but in autumn seeds and grain are eaten. Bobolinks may be attracted to grain scattered on the ground.

NESTING A flimsy nest of coarse grass and weed stems is built in dense grass.

Nesting information *May through July • 1 brood • 5 or 6 pale gray to brown eggs, blotched with brown, purple, and lavender • 13 days incubation by the female • 10 to 14 days fledging*

Blackbird family (EMBERIZIDAE)

RED-WINGED BLACKBIRD

Agelaius phoeniceus
Length: 8¾ inches
(22 centimeters)

The epaulets are displayed in courtship

FROM FALL UNTIL nesting begins, red-winged blackbirds live in large flocks. They spend the night in a communal roost and fly out together in search of food. A visit from a flock can devastate the contents of a feeder. The main habitats are marshes and pastures, but "red-wings" are common in parks and suburban areas, especially as they learn to come to feeders. This is also the probable reason for more red-wings remaining in northern states through the winter.

PLUMAGE The male is black with yellow-edged red epaulets, which may be hidden when perched. The female is streaked brown, with a faint red tinge on the shoulders and sometimes a pink throat. The epaulets of the Californian form lack the yellow edges, and those of the tricolored blackbird (*Agelaius tricolor*) are white-edged.

VOICE The most common calls are loud *chack* notes, given especially when disturbed or flying in flocks. The song is a repeated, liquid *onk-la-reee* or *o-ka-leee*.

FEEDING Red-wings search the ground for seeds and insects. More insects are eaten in the summer.
The red-wing visits feeders for bread, cracked corn, and seeds.

NESTING Red-wings are among the first birds to fly north. The males arrive early, and will attack passing hawks and crows. The nest is a loosely woven cup bound to the stems of cattails, rushes, or other plants, often in marshes and over water.

Gregarious bird In winter, flocks mix with other birds to feed on weed seeds and grain.

Nesting information March through July • 2 broods • 4 blue-green eggs spotted with black and brown • 11 to 12 days incubation by the female • 10 to 12 days fledging

Blackbird family (EMBERIZIDAE)

WESTERN MEADOWLARK

Sturnella neglecta

Length: 9 inches (23 centimeters)

In flight, bursts of flapping alternate with short glides

BOTH THE WESTERN meadowlark and its cousin the eastern meadowlark *(Sturnella magna)* live in open grasslands, but they are adapting to yards. The western meadowlark prefers a drier habitat than the eastern species, but this does not keep them apart, and when they live in the same area interbreeding sometimes occurs. There are some slight differences in plumage, but the best way to tell the species apart is by their songs.

PLUMAGE Slightly paler than its eastern counterpart, the western meadowlark is streaked light and dark brown above, with

Dependent young *Unlike many ground birds, meadowlarks hatch naked and helpless.*

white outer tail feathers that flash when the bird takes off. The breast is clear yellow marked with a broad black V.

VOICE The western meadowlark's song is flutelike and gurgling, while that of the eastern species is a plaintive whistle that sounds like *spring is here.*

FEEDING The main diet is insects, especially locusts, and grain. Meadowlarks are attracted to scattered grain, especially in bad weather, and some will come to elevated feeders.

NESTING The female constructs a dome of grass with a side entrance over a scrape in the ground.

Nesting information April through August • 2 broods • 3 to 7 eggs of white or pink, speckled with brown and lavender • 13 to 14 days incubation by the female • 11 to 12 days fledging

Blackbird family (EMBERIZIDAE)

COMMON GRACKLE

Quiscalus quiscula
Length: 12½ inches (32 centimeters)

The back may reflect bronze, purple, or green highlights

THESE GREGARIOUS birds nest in loose colonies and roost in thousands, often with starlings *(see page 93),* red-winged blackbirds *(see page 112),* and other birds. Common grackles are spreading northward, as are boat-tailed and great-tailed grackles *(Quiscalus major* and *Quiscalus mexicanus).* There are also an increasing number of spring sightings of the common grackle on the west coast.

PLUMAGE The male has all black plumage, with a glossy sheen of purple or bronze, which can be seen in bright light or at close quarters. The purple color is seen over most of the bird's range, north and west of the Appalachian chain, and the bronze is found in the southeast of the United States. The female is duller and has a shorter tail than the male, and the juvenile is dark brown. The eyes of all forms are yellow. Both the boat-tailed and the great-tailed grackles are much larger than the common grackle, with longer tails, and females are lighter brown.

VOICE The call is a loud *chuck.* The song is a harsh squeak, like a rusty hinge.

FEEDING Grackles eat a remarkably wide variety of plant and animal food, gleaned both on open land and in woodlands. They feed on acorns, seeds, and fruit, and can be a pest in grain crops. They take any insects that they can find, probe the ground for earthworms, wade into water to hunt fish and frogs, raid other birds' nests, and even catch bats and birds in the air.

Migrating grackles will descend on feeders in flocks. Grackles are unpopular at feeders because they oust weaker birds. They avidly feed on sunflower seeds and soon finish the supplies. Crusts of bread and kitchen scraps can be used to divert them.

NESTING Grackles nest in loose colonies wherever possible. The nest is a bulky mass of twigs, grass, and mud, lined with more grass, feathers, rags, and string. It is usually built in a coniferous tree or shrub, or sometimes in a building or the bulk of an old osprey nest. Grackles have adapted well to the conditions of human settlement, moving from their original marshy woodland habitats into urban and suburban areas.

Nesting information March through June • 1 brood • 5 or 6 light green or brown eggs with dark-brown blotches • 13 to 14 days incubation by the female • 18 to 20 days fledging

Blackbird family (EMBERIZIDAE)

BROWN-HEADED COWBIRD
Molothrus ater
Length: 7½ inches (19 centimeters)

COWBIRDS ARE NAMED for their habit of following cattle to catch the insects that the mammals stir up from the grass. The birds originally followed bison but switched to cows when herds of cattle replaced bison on the plains. Many people do not welcome cowbirds into their yards, because they arrive in flocks and quickly devour food put out for smaller, more colorful birds. Cowbirds are also disliked because of their unusual nesting habits.

The beak is conical

PLUMAGE The male is glossy black with a brown head. The female is gray-brown above, and paler below. Juveniles are streaked below and scaly above. In the fall, juvenile males are a patchwork of black and brown.

VOICE The calls are a range of rattles and whistles, the song a bubbling gurgle.

FEEDING The main food is seeds, with some fruit. Many insects are also eaten. Bread, cracked corn, and sunflower seeds are taken in the yard.

NESTING Cowbirds are nest parasites: they do not build nests but lay their eggs in other birds' nests. The cowbird finds a nest where the parent bird is laying and slips in an egg of her own. Often the foster parent ejects the strange egg or abandons her clutch to start a new one. If the cowbird egg is accepted, it hatches sooner than the others, and the cowbird nestling outgrows its nestmates.

Prospecting *A cowbird sizes up a cardinal's nest as a possible foster home for her eggs.*

Nesting information 10 to 12 white-brown speckled eggs (usually 1 per host nest) • 11 to 12 days incubation by host species

Blackbird family (EMBERIZIDAE)

NORTHERN ORIOLE

Icterus galbula

Length: 8¾ inches (22 centimeters)

The orange cheeks show that this is a Bullock's oriole

UNTIL RECENTLY THERE were thought to be two similar species of oriole: the Baltimore in the east and Bullock's in the west. Ornithologists now believe that these are subspecies of a single species, the northern oriole. The two interbreed where their ranges meet on the Great Plains. Northern orioles live in open woods, and they have adapted to yards, parks, and avenues of trees along streets. Most migrate to tropical America for the winter, but a few remain behind and feed in yards.

PLUMAGE Males are black above and orange below, with orange on the rump and tail. The Bullock's oriole has a white patch on its wing and orange cheeks. Females are olive and pale yellow. The orchard oriole *(Icterus spurius)* is chestnut, and Scott's oriole *(Icterus parisorum)* has a larger black "hood."

VOICE The Baltimore's call is *hew-li*, repeated in the song. Bullock's oriole has a similar song, but its call is a sharp *skip.*

FEEDING The main food is insects, but fruit and nectar are also eaten. In winter, orioles are attracted to oranges, apples, and jelly. In summer, they visit sugar-water feeders that have perches.

NESTING A pouch of plant fibers, hair, and plant down bound with spider webs is hung from the tips of twigs of large trees.

Putting out short lengths of horsehair and odd pieces of yarn may entice orioles to nest nearby.

Hanging around *A female Baltimore oriole at the nest, which may take two weeks to build.*

Nesting information May through June • 1 brood • 4 streaked and blotched, gray-white eggs
12 to 14 days incubation by the female • 12 to 14 days fledging

Finch family (FRINGILLIDAE)

PINE GROSBEAK
Pinicola enucleator
Length: 9 inches (23 centimeters)

During nesting, the throat develops pouches for carrying food to the young

NOT USUALLY MIGRATORY, preferring to stay in its northern home throughout the year, the pine grosbeak is sometimes forced south by a shortage of seeds, its main food source, and wild fruit. Pine grosbeaks are gregarious birds, living in flocks of up to 100 birds, and they arrive in southern areas in these flocks, seeking coniferous forests, open hillsides, and yards with fruit trees.

PLUMAGE This is the largest of the grosbeaks, with the characteristic heavy conical bill that gives them their name. The male is red, varying from deep rose to bright poppy in color, and has dark wings with two white bars, and a dark, slightly forked tail. It is similar at first glance to the smaller white-winged crossbill (*Loxia leucoptera*). The female is grayish overall, with the same dark tail and barred wings as the male.

VOICE The song is a short, clear, musical warble, including *tee-tee-tew* notes.

FEEDING Pine grosbeaks usually forage for seeds in trees, but also feed on fruit, insects, and seeds on the ground, and tree buds, especially maple buds. Sunflower seed and grain scattered on the ground will attract pine grosbeaks, as will tree-dried fruit such as crabapples and mountain ash and hawthorn berries. They are very approachable at feeders in winter.

Favorite food In winter, pine grosbeaks feed on fruit, especially mountain ash.

NESTING A bulky, loose, open nest of twigs and rootlets, lined with lichens, is built in a spruce, fir, or shrub. Nests in the southern part of the range may be built higher up, because the trees are taller.

Nesting information May through June • 1 brood • 2 to 6 blue-green or gray-green eggs, speckled with brown and gray • 13 to 14 days incubation by the female • 20 days fledging

Finch family (FRINGILLIDAE)

PURPLE FINCH

Carpodacus purpureus
Length: 6 inches (15 centimeters)

In courtship displays the wings are beaten rapidly until they become a blur

THE PURPLE FINCH could be described as the "country cousin" of the house finch *(see opposite)*. It spends most of its time in woodlands, but it will come into suburban areas and take advantage of feeders during the winter. Except when they are nesting, purple finches live in nomadic flocks. These descend on a backyard for a short time and then move on, perhaps not to be seen again until the next winter. Because the house finch is so similar in appearance, very careful examination may be needed to confirm that it is a purple finch flock that has arrived.

PLUMAGE The male purple finch is a softer color than the male house finch. He also has more red coloring overall, but this does not develop until the bird is in its second year. He also lacks the heavily streaked flanks of the house finch. The female purple finch is brown above and streaked below. A white stripe over the eye and dark cheeks and ear patches distinguish her from the female house finch. The male Cassin's finch *(Carpodacus cassinii)* has a brown back, and the female lacks the eye stripe.

VOICE The calls are a sharp, metallic *tick*, which is given in flight, and a musical *chur-lee*. The rapid, warbling song resembles that of the house finch, but lacks the harsh final notes.

FEEDING The diet consists mainly of seeds, especially tree seeds, plus buds in the spring and berries in the fall. Some insects are also taken, and nestlings are fed insects.
Purple finches are frequent but erratic visitors to feeders. They come to all kinds of feeders, but prefer those that are quite high off the ground. Sunflower and thistle seeds are the most popular foods, but other seeds, and suet, are also accepted.

NESTING In the breeding season, purple finches retreat from the yard, mainly to coniferous woods. They build in the outer foliage of trees. The nests are cups of tightly woven grasses, fine twigs, and bark strips (cedar is especially favored) lined with mosses, fine grass, and hair.

Nesting information April through July • 1 or 2 broods • 4 or 5 pale-green eggs with brown speckles • 13 days incubation by the female • 14 days fledging

Finch family (FRINGILLIDAE)

HOUSE FINCH

Carpodacus mexicanus
Length: 6 inches (15 centimeters)

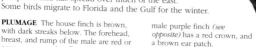

Streaked flanks distinguish this from the purple finch

THE HOUSE FINCH has habits similar to those of the house sparrow *(see page 125)*, and thrives around human habitation. It is not as aggressive as the house sparrow but is popular because of its colorful plumage and melodious song. The house finch is native to the west (where it is called the linnet), but in the 1940s pet dealers in New York imported the birds to sell them as "Hollywood finches." When this came to the attention of the authorities, some dealers released the finches to avoid charges. The species prospered and has spread over much of the east. Some birds migrate to Florida and the Gulf for the winter.

PLUMAGE The house finch is brown, with dark streaks below. The forehead, breast, and rump of the male are red or orange, or occasionally yellow. Cassin's finch *(Carpodacus cassinii)* has a red crown, but is paler on the breast, and the male purple finch *(see opposite)* has a red crown, and a brown ear patch.

Invisible bird These house finches feeding on seeds in winter are excellently camouflaged.

VOICE The call is a *chirp* or *queet* similar to that of the house sparrow. The song is a hurried, repeated warble, ending with a harsh *chee-ur*.

FEEDING Most of the diet is weed seeds, but buds, insects, and scraps are eaten. The house finch eats seeds, peanuts, fruit, suet, and kitchen scraps. It competes with hummingbirds at sugar-water feeders.

NESTING The nest of grasses, leaves, twigs, string, wool, and other odds and ends may be built in a tree, cactus, building cavity, or an abandoned nest House finches use standard nestboxes and may take over purple martin houses.

Nesting information March through August • 1 brood • 4 or 5 blue-white eggs, speckled with brown • 12 to 16 days incubation by the female • 11 to 19 days fledging

Finch family (FRINGILLIDAE)

RED CROSSBILL

Loxia curvirostra

Length: 5½–6½ inches
(14–16.5 centimeters)

Rᴇᴅ ᴄʀᴏssʙɪʟʟs
and the closely related
white-winged crossbills (*Loxia
leucoptera*) have crossed tips to the
bill, for removing seeds from cones.
Crossbills nest when and where they
find crops; they are nomadic and erratic in
their nesting times, because coniferous
trees seed at varying times in different
areas. Outside forests, crossbills are
best known as winter birds. They often
go unnoticed unless you listen for calls,
or look for opened cones on the ground.

*Only two North
American birds
have a crossed bill*

PLUMAGE The male is brick red, darker
on the rump, with dark brown wings and
tail. The female is mottled buff yellow with
dusky wings and tail. Immature males
resemble the females but have touches of
red on the crown. The male white-winged
crossbill is paler, the female less mottled.
Both sexes have two white wing bars.

First bite *A crossbill manipulates a hemlock
cone to get a good grip on it.*

VOICE Flocks of crossbills utter low
twitters to one another when feeding.
During courtship, the male whistles and
warbles from a perch in a treetop or sings
while flying in circles around the female.

FEEDING The cones of pines and spruces
are wrenched from branches and held in
one foot. The crossed bill is used to hold
the scales open while the seeds are
extracted with the tongue. The seeds of
willows, birches, maples, and other trees
are also eaten, as well as some insects.
Crossbills come to sunflower and thistle
seed and sometimes to sources of salt.

NESTING The nest is built well out on a
branch. It is constructed from twigs,
rootlets, and bark, and lined with fine
grasses, moss, feathers, and fur. The
nestlings hatch with normal bills, and the
crossed tips develop slowly.

Nesting information *January through August • 1 brood • 3 to 5 pale blue or green eggs,
marked with browns and black • 12 to 14 days incubation by the female • 17 days fledging*

Finch family (FRINGILLIDAE)

COMMON REDPOLL
Carduelis flammea
Length: 5–5½ inches (13–14 centimeters)

A BIRD OF NORTHERN tundra and coniferous forests, the common redpoll is best-known as a winter visitor. The numbers arriving in southern Canada and the northern United States vary from winter to winter: in some years few appear, in others there is an irruption. Redpolls often seem oblivious to humans, and can become very tame at feeders. Occasionally, a paler redpoll is seen: this is the hoary redpoll *(Carduelis hornemanni)*, which some ornithologists believe belongs to the same species.

The streaked rump distinguishes this from the hoary redpoll

PLUMAGE Common redpolls are streaked gray and brown above, with a red cap, black chin, and pink rump. The underparts are heavily streaked, and some males have a red breast. The hoary redpoll has a shorter bill and is white on the face, rump, and underparts, with a slight pink tinge on the breast.

VOICE The call note is a *swee-e-ee*, coarser than that of the goldfinch. A subdued but constant twitter of lisping notes comes from flocks, and males in flocks sing a junco-like song.

FEEDING The diet consists of buds, seeds from cones, weed and grass seeds, and insects in summer.
Redpolls visit hanging feeders and shelves. They take suet, breadcrumbs, and a variety of seeds, especially niger seeds. They cannot open the hulls of sunflower seeds but take hearts or peck the crumbs left by other birds.

NESTING The female builds a loose cup of twigs, rootlets, grass, and moss, sometimes lined with a layer of ptarmigan feathers, in the crotch of a tree. Several nests may be built quite close together.

Invading forces *Redpolls form into flocks in winter and may irrupt into areas with feeders.*

Nesting information *April through August • 1 or 2 broods • 4 to 7 greenish blue eggs, spotted and lined with purple • 10 to 11 days incubation by the female • 12 days fledging*

Finch family (FRINGILLIDAE)
PINE SISKIN
Carduelis pinus
Length: 5 inches (13 centimeters)

A BOLD BIRD, the pine siskin has no set migration pattern, but wanders the country in flocks of 100 to 200 birds, mixed with other finches. It frequently comes to feeders, where it uses a wings-spread, bill-gaping threat display to chase off other birds.

Compared with other finches, pine siskins are swift, high fliers

PLUMAGE The plumage is gray-brown with conspicuous streaking. The yellow patches on the wings and the base of the tail are most conspicuous in flight, or when giving a threat display with the wings spread. The juvenile has a yellow tinge overall. The closely related goldfinch (*see opposite*) is brighter yellow overall.

VOICE The calls include a long *sweee*, a harsh buzzing *zzzzzz*, and a *tit-ti-tit* given in flight. The song is a trilling warble, which includes the *zzzzzz* and *sweee* notes, given in flight or from a perch.

FEEDING Pine siskins feed mainly on seeds extracted from trees and weeds, or picked from the ground, although they also include insects in their diet, mainly in the summer. They also eat buds and sometimes sip nectar from flowers and sap from sapsucker holes. Ashes and salt put on icy roads and drives in winter are often eaten for their grit and mineral content. Nuts, rolled oats, and a variety of seeds, especially thistle, are taken from feeders.

NESTING Courtship starts toward the end of winter, while the birds are still in flocks. There is a lot of chasing, and the males present seeds to females or flutter in circles singing, with tails spread. Several pairs usually nest together in a loose colony in trees. The females build shallow nests of twigs, grass, and rootlets, lined with fur and feathers.

Party booking *Pine siskins are frequent visitors to feeders, often arriving in large flocks.*

Nesting information April through July • 1 or 2 broods • 3 or 4 green-blue eggs spotted with black • 13 days incubation by the female • 15 days fledging

Finch family (FRINGILLIDAE)

AMERICAN GOLDFINCH

Carduelis tristis

Length: 5 inches (13 centimeters)

The yellow plumage is molted after nesting

THE AMERICAN goldfinch is closely related to the less colorful pine siskin *(see opposite)*, and the two species are very alike in their general behavior. This may lead to competition, and it is unusual to see both birds at the feeder at the same time. One remarkable trait of the goldfinch is that it molts its feathers twice a year: in fall after nesting is completed and again in spring. This results in a great difference in the appearance of the males between summer and winter.

PLUMAGE The winter plumage of both sexes is a brownish gray, but the male has yellow on the throat and face. In spring, the male becomes brilliant yellow, with a black cap, wings, and tail, and white at the base of the tail. The female acquires a yellow tinge but is still quite drab.

VOICE The calls include a *per-chick-o-ree* and, in flight, a *see-me, see-me*. The song is a medley of trills and *swee* notes.

FEEDING Tree seeds, thistles, dandelions, evening primrose, sunflowers, goldenrod, lettuce, and other plants that have gone to seed are the main foods. Berries and insects make up a small part of the diet. Feeders with seeds, especially thistle and sunflower, are popular.

NESTING Loose colonies nest in bushes or trees. The cup nests are sometimes so tightly woven that they can hold water. Nesting is connected with thistles, because the nest is often lined with thistledown.

Solid food Partly digested thistle seeds are fed to the nestlings.

Nesting information June through September • 1 brood • 4 or 5 pale blue eggs • 12 to 14 days incubation by the female • 10 to 16 days fledging

Finch family (FRINGILLIDAE)

EVENING GROSBEAK

Coccothraustes vespertinus

Length: 8 inches (20 centimeters)

The bill becomes green in spring

I N WINTER THE arrival of a flock of evening grosbeaks in your yard is a magnificent and colorful sight, but they can very quickly empty even the largest feeder. The flocks are nomadic, gathering wherever there are good crops of tree seeds, so you may find plenty of evening grosbeaks in your neighborhood one year and none the next. Once confined to the coniferous forests of the northwest, the evening grosbeak spread eastward to the Atlantic coast in the second half of the nineteenth century, and it visits as far south as the Gulf states in the winter.

PLUMAGE The male has a dark brown and yellow body with black wings and tail, a white patch on the inner wings, and a bright yellow line over the eye. The female is grayish without the yellow eye line, but has two white patches on the wings.

Easy pickings *Feeders are popular with evening grosbeaks, although the birds are highly unpredictable visitors.*

VOICE Evening grosbeaks give a variety of *chip* notes almost constantly. The call is *peeear*, and the song a brief warble.

FEEDING The main food is tree seeds – the bird's bill is strong enough to crack cherry pits. Planting of box elder may have helped the bird's spread; the seeds are a favorite food. Flocks gather at roadsides and on driveways to eat grit and salt. Sunflower seed is popular.

NESTING The preliminaries to breeding include the male feeding the female and swinging back and forth with wings spread and quivering. Later stages are hard to observe because the nests, shallow cups of twigs and rootlets built by the female, are well hidden in the foliage of trees.

Nesting information May through July • 1 brood • 3 or 4 blue eggs • 12 to 14 days incubation by the female • 13 to 14 days fledging

Sparrow family (PASSERIDAE)

HOUSE SPARROW

Passer domesticus
Length 5¾ inches (14.5 centimeters)

The wings are drooped to the ground in courtship displays

THE HABIT OF nesting near human settlements has enabled house sparrows, also called English sparrows, to spread over the world. They were introduced into New York in the nineteenth century.

PLUMAGE The male is brown streaked with black above, with gray cheeks, crown, underparts, and rump. The throat and bib are black. The female is more uniformly brown, lacking the gray on the rump and crown and the black on the head and throat. Juveniles are like the female. Some native sparrows are similar but have more slender bills.

VOICE There are various *cheep* and *chirp* calls, and the song is a medley of these.

FEEDING The house sparrow is basically a seedeater, but it will eat a wide variety of food, including shoots, flowers, and insects. House sparrows can be pests on farms, where they will steal grain from standing crops, and in warehouses, railway depots, and other buildings. Urban house sparrows do very well on edible litter and garbage. Spiders and insects are needed for the nestlings.
House sparrows often come to feeders, being quick to learn new ways of finding food. Many make a good living from food put out for birds in yards and parks.

NESTING In spring, several males will chase each other chirping wildly, and mill about, apparently fighting. The object of the fuss is one female, who fends the suitors off, aided by her chosen mate. The nest may be no more than a lining of feathers brought by both sexes, and is used through the winter. The young birds roost together in evergreens and vines. House sparrows readily use enclosed nestboxes *(see page 37)* and may displace native birds.

Close to home *The usual nesting site is a hole or crevice in a building.*

Nesting information April through September • 2 or 3 broods • 4 or 5 white or pale green eggs with a few brown blotches • 14 days incubation mainly by the female • 15 days fledging

· INDEX ·

Acknowledgments

Author's acknowledgments
I would like to thank, in
particular, Gerry Bertrand and
Simon Perkins of Massachusetts
Audubon Society for their
unstinting advice on the habits of
backyard birds, and Arthur
Brown for information on
birdfeeder equipment. I am also
very grateful to the following for
hospitality: Doug and Barbara
Flack, Don Hill, Cathy Yandell,
the Schiefflein family, Gerry and
Faith Bertrand, Joel Rosenbaum
and Connie Drysdale, and Flo
McBride. Everyone helped to
make my stay in the United States
extremely memorable.

Dorling Kindersley Ltd. would
like to thank the following
people for their help during the
preparation of this book: Alison
Anholt-White for coordinating the
North American photography,
Gerry Bertrand of Massachusetts
Audubon Society for advice, and
all who worked on the RSPB
Birdfeeder Handbook.

Dorling Kindersley Inc. would
like to thank the following
people for all their help and
advice: Dr. Susan R. Drennan, Dr.
Stephen W. Kress, and Katherine
Santone of the National Audubon
Society, Deslie Lawrence, and Dr.
Henri Ouellet, National Museum
of Natural Science, Ottawa,
Canada.

PHOTOGRAPHY
Abbreviations: t=top, c=center,
b=bottom, l=left, r=right

Dorling Kindersley
Alison Anholt-White 73br
Martin Brigdale 28tr **Jane
Burton** 23tr, 54b **Peter
Chadwick** 43 **Alan Duns** 28tc
Steve Gorton 16, 21, 22, 23cl,
23br, 24tr, 24cr, 24br, 25bl, 25tr,
25cr, 25br, 26br, 29bl, 31cl, 33br
Dave King 7 **Maslowski Photo**
38bl, 49tl, 51b, 55t, 58, 59b,
62b, 65t, 66b, 68t, 69t, 70t, 76tl,
79b, 81b, 82b, 83b, 83b, 84t, 84b,
85, 86b, 88b, 91b, 94b, 97t, 98t,
100t, 100b, 102t, 103t, 108t, 109t,
109b, 110t, 111t, 113b, 114t, 115b,
116t, 120t, 120b, 121t, 123l
Trevor Melton 24bl **Graham
Miller** 28cr **Kim Taylor** 9bl,
11tr, 11bl, 15br, 17, 18, 19, 20,
25tl, 25cl, 26cl, 26c, 26cr, 26bl,
27, 28tl, 28bl, 28bc, 28br, 29tl,
29c, 29hc, 29br, 32cr, 32bl, 35cl,
36br, 37, 39, 40, 47t, 54t, 75tr, 82t,
92, 125t

Agencies and photographers
Allstock Kim Heacox 63t; Tim
Fitzharris 111b **Animals,
Animals** Richard Kolnar 8
Robert Burton 13tr, 34tl **Bruce
Coleman Ltd.** Robert Carr 15bl;
Jack Dermid 87b; Jeff Foott 31tr;
Wayne Lankinen 61t; Leonard Lee
Rue 34br, 35tr, 116b; John Shaw
15tr **Sharon Cummings** 50, 71t,
112t **Richard Day** 6, 91t, 112t
Frank Lane Picture Agency Ron
Austing 94t, 96b, 124t; Hans
Dieter Brand 65b; Peggy Heard
75b; Daphne Kinzler 33tr; Steve

Maslowski 119b; Roger Tidman
92b; B.S. Turner 125b **J.C. Fuller**
68b, 79t **Russell C. Hansen** 60t,
64t, 74t, 77, 88t, 89t, 90t, 95t
George Harrison 33cr, 42, 49b,
56bl **Imagery** Scott Nielsen
35br, 46t, 53b, 57, 62t, 117t, 121b
Arthur Morris 47b, 53t, 66t
**Natural History Photographic
Agency** R. J. Erwin 13br, 48b,
119t; Steve Krasemann 71b; W.S.
Paton 76b; David Tomlinson 10tr;
Helio Van Ingen 11tr **Oxford
Scientific Films** Jack Dermid
63b; Colin Milkins 9tr; Stan
Osolinski 70b, 90b; James H.
Robinson 99b; Robert A. Tyrrell
30, 59t; Tom Ulrich 104t, 104b
Photo Researchers Inc. Ron
Austing 56r; L. Bachman 107b;
John Bova 64b; Ken Brate 55b,
108b; Robert Carlyle 106b; Joe
DiStefano 60b; Phil Dotson 99t;
Bill Dyer 98b, 101b; Hal Harrison
72b; Harold W. Hoffman 115t;
Steve Krasemann 124b; Leonard
Lee Rue 38tr, 72t; Jeff Lepore
105b; Charles W. Mann 107t;
Thomas W. Martin 106t;
Maslowski 97b; Anthony
Mercieca 67b, 73t, 86t, 96t, 102b,
105t; William H. Mullins 113t; O.
S. Pettingill 95b; William Ray 78b;
Greg Scott 69b; Alvin E. Staffan
87t; Dan Sudia 81t; Joseph Van
Wormer 110b **Leonard Lee Rue
Jr.** 48tr **Ron Sanford** 14, 46b,
122b **Greg Scott** 1, 10tl, 12cr,
12bl, 34cl, 35tl, 74, 80t, 80b, 89h,
103b, 117b, 122t **Hugh P. Smith**
52t, 52b, 61b, 67t, 78t **D.C.
Twichell** 101t **Vireo** S.J. Lang
31br; J.R. Woodward 118t